NINE
STOP
TRIP

By Adam
Byfield

'One Million People Commit Suicide Every Year'
The World Health Organization

Adam Byfield

Published by:
Chipmunkapublishing
PO Box 6872
Brentwood
Essex
CM13 1ZT
United Kingdom

http://www.chipmunkapublishing.com

Proof-read by Lee Kennedy & Takako Kamogawa

NINE STOP TRIP

*For Mum, for Dad
and of course,
for Mary.*

Laura,
It's been a pleasure,
all the best & don't
be a stranger :)

Adam

Adam Byfield

NINE STOP TRIP

OVERTURE

The following trip consists of nine stops at each
of which you will find people struggling to make
sense of the world around them. Some of these
people just need some **TIME TO REFLECT (pg6)** in
order to work out where they stand. For others
it is obsession that poses the problem, when what's
IN THE PICTURE IN THE HOUSE (pg16) becomes more
important than the house itself. You'll find people standing
all alone, their whole world turned against them. Will
they have the strength to hold out until better
times **COME AGAIN (pg29)** ? Maybe not, there are people
along the way who just don't make it, people
who are, in the end, **DEEPDOWNGONE (pg48)** . It can
be so hard to find the time for others
however, when you find yourself too busy at home,
you know how things just **PILE UP (pg70)** . You
will find people who need other people, desperately trying
to turn themselves into **THE i IN TEAM (pg108)** ,
and there'll be others who are just interested in
THE STORY (pg130) , whatever that may be. Some of
the people you will meet on this trip will
be looking for freedom, some will be looking for
BEAUTY (pg147) and there's even one just out for
a good time. Some of them are honest and
kind, some of them are not, and there are
those you wish would just **CUT IT OUT (pg159)** .
There'll be ups, downs and turnarounds. Enjoy the trip.

time to reflect

Author's Note

I already had a copy of Hunter S Thompson's "Hells Angels". It was sleek and smooth with an artistically simple cover and tanned spine; a nice looking book, very modern. So I don't know why I looked up at that shelf that afternoon, but I did, and there it was.

Only the black type of Thompson's name was visible at first, the white letters of the title having faded between the countless breaks in the orange spine. Retrieving the book I thought it might actually come apart in my hands as, unlike most of the stock, it was in pretty bad condition. The cover bore an image of a Hell Angel's leather clad back and the many folds and creases the volume had suffered appeared entirely in place, providing a realism of texture to the biker's jacket.

Having purchased the book, I was flicking through the text when I noticed a brief change in the uniform blur. Turning the pages back carefully, I discovered that, where pages 109 to 116 should have been was, well, something else. The entire ninth chapter had been surgically snipped from the body of the book and replaced with delicate handwritten pages.

I have attempted to reproduce, as faithfully as possible, what appears to be a secret diary. Covering just a few short days, the notes bare no name or date and there is no way to tell when or where the events they record took place. Despite, or perhaps because of this, they provide a disturbing account of life outside both society and sanity.

Adam Byfield,
February 2005,

(This story is dedicated to the
memory of Dr Hunter S Thompson)

NINE STOP TRIP

Day 1

This is not my first day, but it is the first day of these notes. I don't know how many days I have come and sat in this room, it seems like if I'm not sleeping, I'm sitting here, and that's the reason for all this really.

The taking of personal notes is strictly forbidden under the rules of this institution, but I'm losing my mind I'm so bored! I thought recording the day's events might help pass the time, and the fact it's not allowed only adds a little much needed excitement.

My role here is to sit in this dark little room and observe subjects through the broad window before me. When they cast their gazes in my direction, they see only an unbreakable mirror and their own reflections. This doesn't happen very much with my current subject however, as he rarely does very much of anything, hence my utter tedium and ample time for reflection.

While reading on duty is frowned upon, my situation is an apparent exception. I have also carefully dropped into conversation that, because I am reading this novel for my, entirely fictional, book club, I'm annotating it as I go. Hence, amid these little white pages and lies, I have my own space within these walls.

I got here early today to find my subject in his usual, staring heap. He is a young, Caucasian male, just under six feet and would have dark hair if we didn't shave it off. The cotton pyjamas and suede skull are our labels for his illness, the disturbing, self inflicted scars he bares are his own.

The doctors tested him again today, some kind of emotional examination this time. As usual, they both did their best to appear non-threatening. As usual, they failed. No-one was paying me to watch the doctors however, so while I could hear their questions and see their patronising expressions, the arched brows and tightened lips, I ignored them utterly. Against the far wall my subject sat, knees drawn up to his chest, bare feet flat on the floor, staring straight into the mirror.

Watching his pained face closely I found myself feeling increasingly uncomfortable with his treatment. It is vitally important for someone in my position to remain emotionally detached so as to be able to perform their duties, but today, seeing the real fear and real suffering on that man's face, I could not help but feel a deep ache. This was, I realise, a very primal thing, an instinctive desire to reach out and help another human being in need, and this alone I could have forgiven myself and forgotten. What happened next I cannot.

It is true that nurses here are required to wear their hair up, (if it is long,) tight and neat, and that this little room always holds a chill, regardless of the weather outside. Also, if I were one of those nurses who walk around all day I would wear those silly shiny shoes, but as it is, I kick mine off for comfort, despite the aforementioned chill.

Maybe it's not so remarkable then, that, as the doctors were leaving, my subject and I both shuddered at the cold. What disturbed me was the connection I felt to my subject in that moment, as if we shared that shiver. Every time I ask the doctors if I can observe a different subject they just fob me off, but this assignment is really starting to get to me.

Day 2

Nobody noticed that I was late today, or they didn't show if they did. I had a terrible night that left me feeling worse this morning than when I went to bed! I just couldn't seem to settle and while, in the end, I did get more than forty winks, not a one of them was restful.

Arriving, I found my subject to be even less active than usual, having earned himself some sedation with a violent little outburst a few hours earlier. Apparently these incidents occur with some degree of regularity, but I have yet to witness one myself.

The only time I've seen him move today was a few minutes ago actually and, typically, he chose to wait until the one moment I wasn't watching. Being in such a rush and muddle this morning, I forgot all about this wonderful book, (and I was so excited about it yesterday!) and left it in my coat. Several hours of utter stillness had convinced me that it was not only safe, but entirely necessary for me to cross this tiny room and briefly fumble through my coat pocket in order to grab my sanity's lifeline.

Of course this was just when my subject decided to stretch his legs. Cursing him, I moved quickly back to my place, keeping my gaze fixed steadily on that shambling figure. He fidgeted about for a while but settled down again pretty quickly, that's when I started writing this. Well, that's it, nothing to do except watch my subject do nothing. I really hate this.

The doctors visited again this afternoon, but only briefly this time. They said something or other to my subject, but he wasn't listening, I could tell. The true purpose of their visit was the magazine they left behind. Observing the way in which my subject responds to such stimuli is exactly what I'm here for and I hoped that, at last, I might have something to do.

This particular stimulus was a generic men's lifestyle magazine and I watched with interest as, almost immediately, my subject retrieved the glossy heft and began to cast back the pages. As the myriad images flickered by, I found myself torn between looking at my subject's face and the magazine itself.

Those all too familiar features were revealing their first hints of genuine emotion, besides fear and pain, that I could remember seeing. At the same time of course, I had to know which specific images were provoking the various forms of this sudden variety of expression.

My subject passed by the bodies of text and models with a vacant indifference while each one of the abundant advertisements seemed to trigger a mildly disgusted flinch. This, apparently involuntary action, grew in intensity until the tics, knitted together with frustration, became anger.

What was happening before my very tired eyes, and the thought that I may finally see the reported other side of my subject, left me, I uncomfortably admit, giddy. As he tore at the pages I leaned toward the glass, eyes bulging, heart pounding, suddenly drunk with sheer desire, just lusting for something to happen, something to make today different from those before and after.

Then he stopped.

The gaudy cover had boasted of a feature on so called, 'green' cars and it seemed pretty obvious that it was this article that had stopped my subject in his raging tracks. The double page spread that opened the piece was completely occupied by a magnificent treescape. An endless and elegant swarm of slightly different greens thrived from edge to edge, beneath a smooth and brilliant blue.

In the darkness beneath the canopy, pale and tiny letters huddled together to deliver their message, but my subject appeared unaware of the article itself. Instead he simply sat and gazed down into the treetops and sky. The distaste, and subsequent aggressive repulsion of moments earlier, melted away to be replaced by a smile. An actual smile!

The shared shiver of yesterday was a deeply disturbing experience, and yet I found sharing this smile with my subject to be uplifting to the same degree. Why should he care that the Honda Civic 1.3 IMA Executive is considered by some to be the greenest of cars? Or that Peugeot and Citroën are, in the opinion of others, the two greenest car manufacturers?

My subject likes looking at trees. Yesterday I didn't know that, now I do. That's called progress and progress brings change, it leads to endings, new beginnings and most of all, hope.

Day 3

After a much more satisfying night, I arrived right on time this morning feeling something approaching enthusiasm. The tests carried out today would influence future changes to my subject's situation, such as his meds regime or security rating, and so were particularly important.

Showing the doctors just a hint of the positive side I had witnessed yesterday, would have been the first step towards him managing his problems. In light of the intense, and slightly unnerving, connection I had begun to develop with my subject over the past couple of days, I must admit, my hopes were high.

As soon as the doctors entered the room however, I realised that my excitement had been premature. He immediately adopted his usual defensive stance, closing himself off from his visitors. For what seemed like along time, they both sat patiently, describing situations, asking him for an opinion or response. They received neither.

Listening to their words, my own instinctive replies were immediately overshadowed by the obviously correct, or rather obviously sane, responses I knew they were looking for. He just sat however, pathetic and still, hiding in that world of his own. I stared hard at his thin lips, trying to will the words to form, desperate for him not to waste this opportunity, but no, nothing.

The doctors glanced at their watches and then each other and I knew time was running out. Fists, teeth and buttocks clenched, I screamed silently at my subject, demanding he answer the way I knew that he could. As the two pushed him one last time I could see him beginning to grow agitated as his temper rose to meet mine. Seeing this, the white coats retreated before returning with four orderlies.

My subject didn't have the chance to show me his violent side as he was restrained and sedated before having the chance. Watching that tangling heap of bodies my frustrated rage peaked and the sheer hopelessness of it all washed over me.

What can we do? If he doesn't want to be helped, how can we help him? He has to meet us half way, we can't do it for him! This is what I was thinking when I realised what I wasn't feeling. Seeing my subject's pained face the other day, I felt a real sadness. Today, as he was pinned and pricked, I felt no compassion at all. It saddens me to admit it, but it wasn't just necessary, it was deserved.

This is too much, I can't stay here a moment longer, I'm leaving.

Day 4

Well, I came back. I didn't know what else to do. Having left early yesterday I got my head down slept right through to lunchtime today, recent events apparently taking their toll. Today however, I feel worse than ever, having had another restless night.

It does appear I've got away with my lax timekeeping yet again, but I know I can't make a habit of it. Thankfully the doctors won't be visiting my subject today so I can relax a little. Apparently, after the initial sedation wore off yesterday, he erupted into his most violent episode so far. Two whole teams of orderlies came in with both doctors and it was quite a struggle to deliver the required injection and strap him down.

The punches he threw split and bruised his knuckles but, to the credit of the staff, my subject emerged otherwise unscathed from the incident, even though several of the orderlies received fairly serious injuries themselves.

If the frustration of yesterday smashed my sympathy, the news of this outburst has swept it away. Society must be protected from this loser. He make's not the slightest effort towards anything but perpetuating pain, his own and that of others.

He was staring into the mirror today and, for a little while, it seemed he could see me. I knew of course that it was a coincidence and that if I just moved one way or the other his gaze would remain fixed and the illusion would be broken. All the same, I didn't move, I just sat and held his unknowing gaze, wondering how I ever felt any connection with this sad little man. I'll finish now because writing in this awkward little book is giving me terrible cramp in my hands.

Day 5

Everything is different now. These notes were never intended to be read by anyone else in order to lend them a certain magic. Having read the previous pages however, pure shame is now secrecy's motive. I looked through the mirror again today, into those eyes so distant yet familiar. I stared and he stared back until, suddenly, there was something new.

Recognition.

I see now that I've been fooling myself, and I understand the true reason for these notes. I thought they were a sanctuary for the very last vestige of me that didn't belong here. I realise now that they are in fact a final record and resting place.

My doctor will visit soon, probably not alone anymore but with the usual pair of orderlies. I'm feeling pretty sleepy again and by the time they arrive I'm sure that, with the exception of these pages, the shambling shell I've been watching, is all that will remain.

Adam Byfield

IN
THE PICTURE
IN THE HOUSE

The familiar, soft sound of post slapping onto the mat drifted down the dusty hall and up the sleeping stairs to where it found its listener. Lying warm and almost unbearably comfortable amid sheets and pillows, the one man audience opened blurry eyes and stared at the ceiling, pondering what may now await him on the floor below.

A list of wonderful possibilities arose through his slowly broadening consciousness. As reality slowly drew him further away from sleep, however, common sense began to revise and edit this list. Sighing he had initially thought of what should be downstairs on the mat, namely opportunity, luck and/or fortune. Then, with a stretch, a minor chilled grabbed at his naked stomach and prompted thoughts of what could be; demands, bad news, forgotten problems.

Swinging his legs out of horizontal warmth and into the cool morning vertical, his now fully awake mind rested on what he knew was really down the stairs and along the hall. Nothing but veiled tricks, unwanted information and various other wastes of paper. Carrying this grey view he ambled through his morning routine which culminated, some thirteen minutes later, in breakfast with a still mildly hopeful examination of the post.

Five pieces hung from his right hand

awaiting the justification of being read, while he poured the riskily matured milk over his cereal. The first two were dismissed unopened as their envelopes showed them to contain credit card application forms. A pile for the attention of the kitchen bin was created beside the empty milk bottle.

The third piece was a brown envelope with a window and so instantly went onto its own, 'later' pile. The fourth was plain white, a slightly different shape to the others and strangely smooth. Leaving his spoon to its milky bath he eagerly tore into this possible opportunity, luck and/or fortune. As soon as the corner of the enclosed letter became visible, however, he knew that this piece too was destined to lay with vegetable peelings and egg shells. Annoyed at having his hopes raised and feeling a little stupid for allowing them to be, he tore rashly into the final envelope.

So rash was he, in fact, that the contents leapt spitefully from the brown paper only to float gracefully beneath the kitchen table. After a string of grumbled expletives and the groan of his chair as he pushed it back a hand appeared under the table. Minimal groping time later and his fingers happened upon what had fallen from the envelope. Frowning, he sat back into his chair and unfolded what appeared to be a piece of shiny white card. It had been bent roughly in two so as to fit into the envelope.

Flattening it out he realised that it was in fact a large colour photograph. Glancing around and examining the remains of the brown envelope he could find no accompanying note or caption. His milk and cereal forgotten, left to form a new single mass within the bowl, he felt the thrill of something different captivate him as he studied the photograph.

The scene was indoors and slightly disturbing in its apparent journalistic style. A middle aged woman wearing an apron was charging towards the camera wielding an axe, two handed, over her head. Below the axe her light brown hair stood in frozen swirls suggesting that the unkempt bun atop her head was about to fall.

Her mouth and eyes were wide and it was the reality of her expression that made the observer uncomfortable. The light that reflected up from the gloss surface of the photo seemed to carry with it an echo of pure hatred and unrestrained malice. The photo itself almost seemed to vibrate slightly with the sheer force of the violence captured in that moment.

The woman was framed by an open doorway through which she had obvious arrived at some speed. It was possible to make out enough of the room beyond to note that the décor seemed to be in keeping with that of the foreground. Dark wooden panelling and antique furniture suggested that the house was rich in both age and material wealth. In fact, minus the crazed axe woman, the house appeared to be a sleepy stately home.

Having stared into the manic face and examined its surroundings he realised that he was enjoying the discomfort the photograph stirred within him. The subtle unpleasantness and creeping dread that seemed to give it unnatural weight thrilled him. A vague sense of danger quickened his breath and suddenly he felt he was actually living his life, instead of just watching it, for the first time in a long time.

His newfound connection with his environment was quickly broken however as he glanced over at the clock. Each movement of the second hand was as the crack of a whip now that the minute hand had moved beyond the hour and he was late for work. Quickly arranging the photograph and most of its envelope in a pile of their own he left the kitchen and then the house.

Over the next two weeks he returned to the photograph several times, studying it anew and trying to familiarise himself with every detail and nuance.

The power of the scene had lessened very little since that fateful morning, and that first glimpse had planted a seed of desire that had cut through the boredom that swamped his mind. This once instant held so much passion and energy that he longed to know of the moments fore and aft. So many blank labels hung from the image demanding names, motives and consequences.

He had placed the photograph and envelope into a larger envelope to keep them safe and together. Within this envelope they lay quietly next to a single sheet of paper that bore a list of names.

Adam Byfield

Each time he removed this piece of paper from the envelope he felt a little ridiculous. The day after he had received the photograph he had examined the post mark on the envelope and then, using his road atlas, made a list of the stately homes within that area. Only upon completing the list after a very satisfying hour of work, did it occur to him that the *photo* of the house had not necessarily been posted anywhere near the *actual* house.

Still he was compelled to interrogate his life's most interesting parcel for clues as to the incident caught so graphically, and apparently for his benefit, on film. Frustration, however, at his inability to make further progress began to interfere with the experience of viewing the photograph itself. It was at the end of these two weeks that he put his project in a drawer and left to visit his family for the festive season, determined not to think of it again.

He proceeded as planned until the latter half of Christmas day when he found himself sat around the extended table with his extended family. Wearing a paper crown he extracted the rest of what his cracker had to offer. A small plastic elephant and a folded piece of paper presumably carrying a joke were his prizes. Arching his arm over his bright green crown he scratched his head in a rather simian fashion and drank the rest of the wine in his glass.

After a precarious refill operation he turned his attention back to his joke. His fingers seemed too big and thick to open the small folds of paper and once he had the revealed writing was blurred.

NINE STOP TRIP

A moment's concentration brought the letters into some semblance of focus.

Q. *"What do call a dead photographer?"*

A. *"Anything you like, he can't hear you!"*

He dropped the slip as if it were red hot. A single gasp of air seemed to wash any stupor instantly from his system, leaving him cold and still. The joke had fallen face down onto the even whiter tablecloth and he couldn't bring himself to touch it again to confirm what he was sure he had seen.

After a moment he looked around quickly, wondering if any of his relatives had noticed his reaction. Everyone seemed to be quite merry in their own conversations and/or consumptions with exception of his young nephew. Sitting directly to his right, his nephew had only recently started attending school and was looking at him with two great question marks for eyes.

"What was in your then?" he asked, motioning towards the boy's cracker. Still considering his uncle with suspicion his nephew began to empty his own cracker remnant. After the discovery of a hat, followed by the trading of hats, the boy seemed to have forgotten his uncle's strange reaction and was eager to enlist his help with the reading of the joke.

After a moments hesitation he was pleased

to discover that his nephew's joke was perfectly normal, very old and not at all funny. With relief he watched the young boy retrieve his final prize, a small plastic magnifying glass. He made some comment about not starting any fires which his nephew ignored, now engrossed as he was in viewing the world through the small plastic lens.

Turning back to his own place setting he expected to again be confronted by the rear of the offending joke however it was not there. The remnant of the cracker was also conspicuously absent however the plastic elephant still sat patiently, now alone on the plain of white cotton, hopeful of some attention.

His family members had cleared some of the debris from the table to make way for yet another course. A spark ignited at the back of his mind and suddenly the fear inspired by the weird joke didn't feel entirely bad. He glanced to his right and watched the light reflect off the lens of his nephew's new toy. A plastic elephant wasn't going to be enough...

In the end he had simply had to wait until his nephew had grown tired and was whisked away by his mother. Back home the photograph was now revealing a whole new level of detail through the plastic lens of a child's toy. The first major leap he made with this new technology was the discovery of a magazine sat on a chair in the far left of the foreground. The cover was a dark purple blue and the title sang out, in bold white letters made legible by the magnifying glass.

Any trace of the shame felt at making the list of stately homes was washed away entirely by his newly discovered passion. A brief spell of research on the internet revealed the contact details of the magazine in question. An even briefer phone conversation told him that the magazine was a mail order only publication for very wealthy book collectors; that edition of the magazine had been published in early December, and that they certainly would not, under any circumstances, furnish him with a list of subscribers and their addresses.

Although he was no closer to finding the house, he now knew that the photograph had been taken only days before he had received it. This alone quickened his pulse but the discovery of the magazine had also caused him to notice the abundance of books on the walls. Checking his list he found that only three stately homes boasted great libraries and quickly located the three on the map.

On some level he was aware of just how tenuous all this was but these doubts were overridden by excitement, by a strange feeling of just *knowing* he was right. The very feeling of belief itself seemed to lift him regardless of what it was in. During a brief pause in his efforts he reflected how easily this mystery had captured his complete devotion, but before he could make any conclusions over what this said about his life he noticed the shadows.

A few days earlier he had noticed a carriage clock and been able to read the face. There appeared to be large windows to the left hand side of the photographer and it was from here that the daylight streamed. He now saw that the woman, still midstride in her homicidal charge, cast a shadow just about visible at the bottom of the photograph directly to the right.

The recently discovered clock said that it was late afternoon; he knew it must be early December, and the light was coming in straight through the window. Before he even had chance to think about it these facts combined themselves into a single new form. The windows must be facing west so the photographer was facing north. Did this help him? He wasn't sure, but the sense of satisfaction he got from adding yet another detail to his picture made it seem worth the effort.

After finding the shadows he again seemed to run out of clues and took to simply looking at the woman's face through the magnifying glass. The utter rage that gleamed in those eyes still fascinated him and, after examining her expression so carefully, he was absolutely convinced that she could not be acting.

New Year came and went and he returned to work, only opening the box file he now kept his *real* work in on weekends. It was a particularly rainy one of these weekends when he discovered the penultimate detail in the photograph. Gazing, once again, at the expression the women had held for over two months now, he noticed the subtle tension of the muscles beneath her skin. Her grimace pulled her neck taught beneath her chin and he was tracing these lines with his eye when he noticed her necklace.

The chain was so thin that it was all but invisible but the small golden ornament that hung from it was not. Though it was mostly hidden from view behind the apron but the top corner of the necklace sat proudly on display. With glee he quickly arranged the rest of his notes and began to try and sketch the tiny visible fragment.

By the time he felt he was confident about the design he had a splitting headache. Staring mercilessly through the small plastic magnifying glass had not done him any direct physical benefit. The feeling of elation, however, when he found that the design appeared to roughly match a crest of one of his three stately homes, meant that he barely even noticed the pain behind his eyes.

Without hesitation he planned his route to the house; put brand new batteries in his brand new digital camera, and called work to leave a message explaining his absence the following day due to sickness. He would find this room, take a picture of his own and then frame them both as a trophy of his achievement in finding one purely from the other. He went to bed earlier than usual but found it difficult to sleep. When sleep finally began to creep over and calm him he did wonder at the intensity of his excitement but this thought quickly melted into dreams.

He approached the great house down an incredibly long, straight and grey driveway flanked by rolls of green. The photo rested heavy in his jacket pocket while the camera hung around his neck as if in imitation of that most recent clue that had brought him here. Queuing and paying and queuing and parking and walking to the house seemed to take forever but eventually he stepped into the building and was immediately thrilled by the familiar décor.

The doors through which the visitors entered were set into the south face of the vast building and he made sure to maintain a solid sense of direction as the tour began. To his annoyance he realised that they were headed in the exact opposite direction to where he was sure the room must be but assumed that they would get to it eventually. As the tour progressed, however, he began to worry that they may not be shown that particular room at all. As it seemed that the tour was about to end he felt something similar to panic begin to grip him.

To come this far, to get this close, he couldn't just walk away. Feigning interest in one particularly large and ugly portrait he allowed the rest of the group to pass him. Then, choosing his moment carefully, he slipped back into the previous room and waited there until the guide's voice had faded to nothing. He felt giddy and an idiot grin held his face. Heart pounding he proceeded with stealth towards the west side of the house. He had never felt so exhilarated, so alive. Holding his camera in his right hand and the photograph in his left his stalked onward. This was real and it was happening to him.

He was so caught up in the sensation, in fact that when he passed through a doorway to be faced by a westerly view he was taken slightly by surprise. He must have overestimated the distance to this side of the house, he supposed, or lost track of how long he had been walking, he admitted.

Turning to the south side of the room he saw only books, floor to ceiling leather bound volumes. Knowing he must be close now his finger rested on the shutter release of the camera. He gripped the photograph and, almost for comfort, raised it to eye level and peered at it intently. His eyes were drawn to a familiar sight, a small blur in the room beyond the axe woman. An ornate wall plaque or something similar he had always thought, but today it appeared in a new light to him.

The feeling rushing through his veins seemed to heighten his senses, everything appeared crisper and more defined. Looking again at the blur he suddenly remembered the first time he had seen two silhouetted faces become a white candlestick. Before his eyes the blur seemed to shift within itself in that same magical fashion and become a mirror. There was a reflection in the mirror, a figure that had formed the blur. He strained his eyes and suddenly he saw it.

The reflection was him, wearing the same jacket he was wearing now. Hearing a noise behind him he turned to the north as his ears were assaulted by a banshee howl. In the same instant he gripped his camera with one hand, pressing the button, while dropping the photograph from the other. He had intended to look to his own reflection in the mirror that he now knew hung in the room before him but his eye was inescapably drawn, as it always was, to the woman with the axe.

COME AGAIN
COME AGAIN
COME AGAIN
COME AGAIN
COME AGAIN

A vast expanse of green billowed out below and undulated to the horizon. As they varied in shade the great emerald arcs were split here and there by dark, rigid divides. The omnipresence of the fluttering blades, however, made the squat, dry stone walls appear as insubstantial surface defects. Occasional trees stood tall and breathed deep the cold open air, gently nodding their contentment.

Over another great rise a wide strip of grey came into view. A dull and sulking ribbon, it lay across the rippling green and stubbornly refused to join the swaying motion that surrounded it. The only sound that just about cut through the sighing of the wind was a dirty cough that spoke of labour and struggle. Desperately clawing its way along the contour of the earth, following the resolute grey ribbon, a small, royal blue truck wheezed and whined.

Its colour was a distant echo of the brilliant blue of the sky above which was saddened here and there by gentle greys. These served only to enhance the sky's blue in its deeper regions and made the shade of the truck to appear as a gaudy and tarnished replica. An insult to its environment, it staggered on a little further.

Leaving the tarmac of the road the truck uttered a desperate squeal as it was driven up onto a dirt track. Amidst the fluid curves of the open moor the truck's tyres tore into the earth and made slow but determined progress towards a small barn that now became visible.

Old twisted planks of wood huddled together and held each others weight as the wind whistled between them. Lacking the flexibility of their previous forms, who still swayed and nodded in the background, they could only creak and groan stiffly with the breeze.

The trucks engine idled but was to find no rest as its driver emerged and approached the barn on foot. The torrents of air immediately fell upon him, lifting his light brown hair up from his scalp to dance on end and join the universal rhythm. While his hair bucked and swayed the rest of him could not be drawn. His movements were violent and purposeful as he removed chain and padlock from the groaning doors and dragged them open.

The truck shuddered as the man leapt back within it, slamming the driver's door in firmly beside him. With a splutter the pair jerked into the minimal shelter of the barn and disappeared from view. After a moment the man appeared briefly to struggle the doors closed. Minutes carried the weight of decades as the wind regained its monopoly on all visible motion.

Having regained their dominance, currents of chilled air tore at the feeble structure and, in an instant managed to tear one its weary doors open.

NINE STOP TRIP

As the door flailed in the gale, hinges screaming, the howling wind plunged vengefully into the barn only to find nothing but shade and space…

He had been talking for about five minutes and so far it was going well. All he had to do was keep reading from the cards he had prepared and he would get through this in no time. The audience's attention was being held and he began to relax a little as he switched to the next card.

2.   *"…I will show that it is the emergence of*

culture that has halted the process of natural
(SNEER)   (PROUD)

selection… We will then go on to see that, as a
        (PAUSE FOR EFFECT)

result, only the most dramatic of mutations could
                                    (EYE CONTACT)

now possibly make a big enough step forward to

produce the competition required for natural

selection. Such mutations are unlikely to occur

naturally however, and so, it is in fact, culture… and
                                                                (PAUSE FOR EFFECT)

its technology that may yet prove to be the catalyst."

3.   *"The radiation that is produced and **supposedly***
(ROLL EYES)

contained by certain areas of military research is a

fine example of an evolutionary accident waiting to

happen. Some such research is undertaken in

startling proximity to the civilian population in

***apparently** secure underground laboratories.*
(SHAKE HEAD, EYEBROWS)

*Anyway having demonstrated the **what** and the **how***
(HANDS)   (HANDS)

*of the **EVOLUTIONARY HIATUS...** we shall finish today*
(LET THEM RECALL TITLE)

*by considering the beliefs of some as to the **who**..."*
(MYSTERIOUS!)

The smooth openness of the table top filled her vision. Feeling acutely aware of the cotton collar of her shirt shifting against her damp neck, she had bowed her head to yet another tirade.

"What's his name? Just tell me his name..." her father's eyes were wild and rolled manically as he paced back and forth beyond the kitchen table. Despite her strongest efforts she could not ignore the angry and pained sounds he had been making for almost half an hour. His words cut into her and dragged her down into sorrow as she saw her mother, from the corner of a wet eye, slumped against the wall. Overcome with emotion, her mother's suddenly frail frame was racked with sobs. As her father came to the end of this latest breath he once more held her weary but full attention.

"Who is it? WHO!?" With this last roar his palms slammed down onto the table, rattling her jaw. For an instant he appeared, across that plain of lightly varnished wood, as a great and terrible sphinx before her. She knew the answer to his riddle but would not tell him. This daydream was abruptly ended by the silence it preceded.

This was her chance. Feeling his stare on her scalp she knew that all she had to do now was say the name, just two simple words, and this would end. Her father would tear from the house on his way to do something terrible and her mother would scold her for the trouble she had caused before grasping her into the weeping, rocking hug of old.

She raised this knowledge along with her head and met her father's pleading gaze. For a moment she saw hope in his eyes and in its light she even saw love. But as the seconds drew out and the silence remained unbroken, hope faded and his eyes clouded with rage.

She noticed she had been holding her breath but continued to do so as her father became very still and underwent a startling transition from ruby red to granite grey. As he raised his left hand to conduct his words she noticed it was shaking slightly.

"Girls," he said hoarsely, "do not fall pregnant by themselves. Especially," his voice rising back towards its former shelf rattling heights, "not a daughter of mine!"

Silence quickly rearranged itself upon the table and she realised that this last statement was to be taken more than just literally. Seeing that she had not understood he barked, "Get out!"

A low cry from her mother swept between them as she searched her fathers ashen features for signs of bluff or regret. His expression was as hard as the rock his complexion now resembled. She held his stare, and him for a second, before he turned from the table and strode to the door.

"But she's your daughter!" screamed her mother desperately.

"I don't have a daughter, and neither do you!" he roared before slamming the door behind him by way of emphasis. Again she stared down at the table, this time accompanied by the sounds of her mother's exhausted tears. She had thought long and hard about this decision, more so than anything else she could think of, but it had never occurred to her that she may never see this table again. Looking out of the window to her left she tried to memorise the rolling green arcs of the view but all she could think of were the packed suitcases upstairs.

6.   *"**Survival... of the fittest!** This... is the law of*
      (PAUSE FOR EFFECT)

   natural selection, though it is worth noting that the

   *word **fittest**... here refers to the **most fitting,** not*
   (LET THEM THINK)   (HANDS)

   *necessarily the **healthiest.** By protecting our weaker*
                    (SMILE)   (SERIOUS)

   brothers we allow their physical weaknesses to

   continue in future generations. Is this a failing or

   simply a new, more conscious approach to

   advancement of the species? No matter! The fact
                          (EYEBROWS)

   remains that we have ceased to evolve physically."

Even though the taste of vomit on his tongue was a constant reminder of the gut wrenching fear he had experienced less than an hour earlier, he was amazed to find that he was actually enjoying giving this lecture. As he switched to the next card he noticed that he was sweating profusely, but he felt good.

7.   *Our state of arrested development on the*

evolutionary ladder leaves us **vulnerable** *to being*
(SCARY)

overtaken. It is feasible to suggest that a **mutant**
(SERIOUS)

could be born with such great advantages over the

rest of humankind as to be the first of a new

species. Depending on the circumstances of the

mutation... **there may be more than one...** *and, if*
(PAUSE FOR EFFECT)

given the chance, *a new dominant race could*
(DIRE WARNING, FINGER)

knock us from this pedestal we have **taken for**
(PASSION)

granted *for so long.*
(FIST)

She had been in the city almost six months when she had read the news story about her small village. Two young women who had fallen pregnant just before she had, had both lost their babies on the same day. One woman, whom she only vaguely knew, had been in a hit and run; while the other, a former school friend, had fallen badly at home.

Immediately she thought to call her friend but then she looked down at her own swollen belly. Everyone in the village knew of her *circumstances* and as a result her friend would probably not appreciate, or even take her call. The story spoke briefly of, *"a village in mourning,"* before concluding with a passing mention of the nearby MoD facility.

With a sigh she turned her attention to preparing dinner for herself. She was staying in a friend's flat which was small, comfortable and conveniently empty due to a business trip to Holland. As much as she tried she couldn't shift the heavy feeling of dread that had seemed to settle over her as she had read the newspaper.

Not since her very first night in the city had she felt quite so vulnerable or alone. As she peeled the potatoes she tried reminding herself that her friend would be back in a couple of days, no doubt laden with gifts and stories. It didn't seem to help.

Carrots now and she knew exactly why she felt as she did. Some idiot street preacher had given her a scare earlier in the day and she'd been on edge ever since. This piece in the paper had just topped it all off. Frowning she recalled what had happened as she had been leaving the market with the vegetables she was now dissecting.

Although, or perhaps because, he was engulfed in a full length black cloak and was screaming passages from an obscure religious text; the busy, consuming public ignored him utterly. She had hurried past him, practicing her new found city social skill of cold indifference.

"You!" he had screeched, his voice cracking to a ridiculously high pitch. Instinctively she had glanced over her shoulder to discover, to her horror, that the maniac was addressing her. His eye's burned amid his weathered face, flushed with religious fervour. With a slight shudder she had turned and hurried away, trying not to hear the screechings that clawed at her heals

"YOU! THE CHERUBIM WHORE! THE DEMONIC VIRGIN!" She had kept walking, cringing all the way. "THE CHILD MUST DIE!!!" This last outburst had been accompanied by a general clatter as the hysterical preacher had collided with a market stall in his stumbling pursuit of her.

Scraping the sliced vegetables from cutting board to pan she frowned as she finally realised just what had been so disturbing about the, quite obviously disturbed, preacher. In those moments of eye contact she had noticed not only genuine recognition in the strange man's eyes but genuine fear as well. He had been terrified, of her. With a shudder she put the days events, experienced and reported, from her mind and flicked on the television, it's gaudy glow a welcome distraction...

She was in bed and she was awake. In the instant that was all she knew. The room was in utter darkness and a thick blanket of silence seemed to lay over her own flimsy bedclothes. Rubbing her right eye with a sleepy finger she pondered what had woken her, and rolled over to find her alarm... *there's someone stood at the foot of the bed!*

Between the horned figure appearing in the corner of her eye and her back hitting the headboard, sheets up under her chin, her mind was blank. She goggled in failing disbelief at the huge goat's head sitting atop the intruder's shoulders as he slowly raised a long arm from within his red robes and pointed to her swollen belly.

"The child must die." The words rumbled and echoed from within the mask before rolling up the bed to push her to the peak of hysterical terror. She was suddenly aware that there were other people in the room, a hand over her face, a strange smell, then…

She was in bed and she was awake. In an instant she was fumbling for the light and casting a wide eyed gaze around the empty room. Taking a deep breath she thought only of the relief she now felt and tried let the nightmare slip away. As her heart slowed she realised that she was lying on sheets warm with fluid. Blushing, she reflected on just how scared she must have been moments earlier before realising that, actually, she had not wet the bed. This water had broken not passed.

For a moment she simply sat and tried not to panic before going into the routine she had practiced so many times over the past few weeks. Minutes later she was crossing the living room to the familiar sound of the bedroom door swinging closed behind her. The bag she had prepared felt heavier now that things were happening for real.

She reached the phone and made the call before turning to sit on the arm of the sofa and resting the bag on the floor. With a sigh she looked up and saw it. Dark red, dripping letters daubed hatefully across the bedroom door.

**THE
CHILD
MUST
DIE**

Her hand was at her mouth, eyes bulging, as the next contraction came…

10.   *For many the idea of mutation conjures up*

***ridiculous** images of cartoon characters with super*
(ROLL EYES)

*powers. We **must** put these images to one side if*
(POINT)

we are to see the true potential, and threat… of
(OMINOUS PAUSE FOR EFFECT)

mutation. Let us consider Albert Einstein's brain… It
(PAUSE FOR LAUGHTER)

is a little known fact that one particular piece of

Einstein's brain was much larger than normal. This

area of the brain deals with abstract and creative

mathematical thought and so this mutation explains

Einstein's genius!

11.   *If a physical mutation can change the face of*

mathematics and science we **must** *consider what*
<small>(HANDS)</small>

other aspects of human society could be

revolutionised *in this way. Let us consider, for*
<small>(DRAMATIC)</small>

example, the spiritual pursuits of mankind. The

prevalence of organised religion throughout history

and across the globe suggests that religious beliefs
<small>(HANDS)</small>

are a fundamental part of being a human being.

Now, what if an individual were born **without** *this*
<small>(MYSTERIOUS)</small>

need for faith in the unseen?

Even though the timetabled laugh had not appeared he still felt he was riding high and was excited as he approached his grand finale. One person had left a few minutes earlier but even this hadn't dented his newfound confidence. Those who remained seemed genuinely interested, some of them were even taking notes!

The events of the previous night still echoed coldly on the sidelines of her thoughts, but the warmth of her newborn son seemed to outshine any mere memories. Sitting upright in her hospital bed she cradled the tiny child and watched adoringly as he slept, entirely oblivious of the impact his arrival had made.

She had still been hysterical by the time she had reached the hospital, so much so that some psychologist or councillor had come and spoken with her. He had seemed a kind, if slightly severe man, and he had explained it all. Silently she repeated his explanation of events, a mental mantra to insulate herself from those cold, lurking images.

Her *circumstances* had put her under a great deal of stress. On some level she had felt a degree of resentment towards her unborn child for causing such upheaval. Feeling guilty about this and especially vulnerable, being practically alone in the city while heavily pregnant, had caused her to have the nightmare and the subsequent hallucination. After all, the paramedics who had found her hadn't mentioned any graffiti or goatsheads, what other explanation was there? It wasn't real, she reminded herself, frowning slightly. He's real though, she thought and as her son wriggled slightly in her arms she could only smile.

Some time later they were disturbed when the door opened and a young nurse entered quietly. Though she was certain that she had not encountered this nurse during her stay at the hospital, the young uniformed woman seemed familiar. She held her son a little closer as their visitor approached and, from behind a polite smile, she tried to remember where she had seen this woman's face before.

NINE STOP TRIP

Reaching the bed the nurse whispered, "time to get you two down to the ward. I'll take him and an orderly will be along for you shortly. You can see him again just as soon as we get you both settled." She smiled again and leaned in to take the child. Still holding her baby tightly, she drew a breath to find it seeped in a strange aroma. The nurse stopped and looked at her, still smiling but now slightly puzzled. Incense, why did the nurse smell of incense? Why did she recognise the incense?

Suddenly she was back in her own bed, in the dark but not alone in the room. As she realised the significance of the smell that had transported her back to the previous night's horror, an expression of terrified recognition hijacked her tired features. In an instant the nurse's entire demeanour shifted.

Her hair seemed to shift back from her brow as her smile was replaced by a cold and cruel expression that hinted towards a sneer. With hard eyes the nurse lunged, making a grab for the boy hissing, "the child must die!".

It was as if she were watching herself act.

She was sure that, at that time, after all she'd been through, there was no way she could have struck the nurse, knocking her to the floor before leaping from the bed and sprinting from the room clutching her son. Despite reason, however, she watched herself do exactly this and before she knew it she was running barefoot down a wet pavement.

The hospital gown she wore barely

protected her modesty let alone her shivering limbs from the cold night air. Her pounding heart left no room for denial or hopes of misunderstanding. Satanists wanted to kill her baby. The words seemed ridiculous yet her situation was anything but. Pausing to postpone the explosion of her burning lungs she looked at her immediate surroundings. Amazingly her son had slept through their flight from the hospital and only now was he roused from his slumber.

Though the pavements were wet the darkened sky had been clear when she had made their escape. As she tried to comfort the child, gasping wildly, drops of rain began to dot the light blue of her gown. Looking around once more she saw it. The only building showing any light did so through a huge and ornate circular window. A church. Thanking a god that she had never believed in, she raced to the heavy wooden doors and began pounding.

Minutes later she and her baby were sat on an old chair, wrapped in a heavy blanket. Attached to her quaking hand the old priest sat calmly and listened with kind eyes as she recounted the entire tale, her hysteria seeming to relish every detail. Eventually she finished and seemed to sink in on herself, down into the folds of the blanket. For a short time the priest simply held her hand and let her breath. When he did speak his voice was quiet and warm.

"There are many people in this world who hold strong spiritual beliefs. Belief can be a very powerful thing, and people will do the most extreme things in it's name. Many of these things are good, my child," he patted her hand and smiled, looking down at the infant in her lap, now fast asleep once more.

"But there are those whose beliefs are not of love. There are people who, through reasons of their own pains in life, choose to put their faith in hatred and the suffering of others but," he paused, catching her drying eyes, "there are very few of them. I have sent Simon to call the police, you will be safe here until they arrive."

Looking at his smiling face and feeling the blanket around her, she felt she could finally breath deeply again. As she was doing so 'Simon' appeared from a shadowed door, the younger man appearing no less compassionate than his senior.

"Father," he addressed the priest quietly, "I found the crib that you asked for."

"Ah yes," he replied before, turning back to her, "we have a crib from last years nativity. I thought you may like to put him down for a few minutes. I'm sure we can find you some dry clothes to wear."

Sniffing a little she became aware of the cold and clinging hospital gown between her and the blanket. Looking from her child to the priest, she found peace in both faces. "Well, just for a little while," she said, reluctantly handing her son to the black clad man. Standing she watched as the old priest handed such a tiny bundle to Simon. "I thought Jesus was born in manger," she said, attempting a smile. After a second's confusion the old man's face cleared and he replied.

"Oh, I see. No, we got a crib so that the little star of our show had somewhere to sleep when offstage." Beaming he put a fatherly arm around her shoulder and lead her from he room.

"Do you see how important your belief has been? Your faith in yourself got you here, and your faith in us has saved you. Faith is such an important part of life, my child, we must do anything we can to keep it alive in the world..."

14.   *Since long before Charles Darwin there has been a*

*legend... a **myth**... or, in the opinion of some... a*
(DRAMATIC PAUSE x2)

*real life **conspiracy!**, concerning just such a*
(EXCITING!)

mutation. According to various sources, it is said
(SERIOUS)

that certain lines were intentionally omitted, not only
(SECRET)

from St.John's "Revelations" in the bible, but from all

major religious texts. The passage spoke of the

coming of a new man... a man who would lead
(DRAMATIC)

people away from gods and into a new age. No
(SERIOUS)

religion could survive the appearance of this man.

NINE STOP TRIP

For some reason, the priest's words stopped her in her tracks. Seemingly unphased by their unscheduled stop, the priest continued.

"And so I hope you now see my child…"

15.   *For this to happen…*
            (PAUSE FOR

"…that is why…"

                        it is essential
                        EFFECT)

"…the child…"

                        the mutant

"…must die."

                        survives.

The four leaden words fell upon her, driving her down into cold and clumsy terror, but already her body was fighting against the priest's kindly restraint…

Adam Byfield

DEEPDOWNGONE

Writing is a curious pastime. It changes the way you see the world, or rather it adds extra dimensions to the world you see, you begin to see writing everywhere. For example, instead of just hearing dialogue on TV, you see familiar language tricks, subtle linguistic techniques employed for a specific practical purpose.

Patterns begin to emerge from everyday life, the mechanics of how people meet and interact, of how situations come together. Just as a doctor comes to see the human body as a fascinating machine, as well as a person, writers develop a similarly detached parallel view of the world around them.

We all occasionally encounter things day to day that are anything but everyday. We come across things that, if they were written as fiction, would be dismissed as simply ridiculous. Despite this however, such events continue to spring from the supposedly mundane real world.

When I heard what had happened to Sean Lofte's wife, and subsequently witnessed the toll it took on him, I was deeply saddened. There was another part of me however, that could see those events only as a darkly fascinating story.

I first met Sean several years ago, back when he'd been seeing a friend of mine. I had also been seeing a guy at the time and the four of us had gone out together for a few months, just a couple of couples enjoying each other's company and conversation.

NINE STOP TRIP

My first impression of him had been of a very intense and possibly pretentious young man. In fact I remember distinctly quizzing my friend in the ladies the first night we all went out together, asking her what she saw in him.

Over the next few weeks however I got to know Sean and came to agree with the answer she gave me that night. He was a passionate guy who just never seemed to stop thinking, but he was genuine and caring and actually, once you got used to him, quite fun to be around.

I never did find out exactly what went wrong with Sean and my friend but their relationship came to an end after a few months. I promptly forgot all about Sean, adding him to a list of brief past acquaintances to be filed somewhere at the back of my mind.

When I heard the breathless tale from my friend last year, I had dearly hoped that there was an element of Chinese to her whispers. The next day however the details were all over the local news and there was no escaping what had happened. We all have bad days from time to time but Sean must have broken some kind of horrible record with this one.

A prolonged and bitter row with his wife over breakfast meant that Sean had arrived late at the office on that wet, grey morning. Finding the car park full, he had been forced to park in a nearby alley and walk. He had finally sat down at his desk only to discover that problems with the company's IT systems meant that much of the work he had produced over the previous few weeks had been lost.

According to the papers, his frustration at the day had stretched his already strained relationship with his boss to breaking point. By late afternoon, in an episode reportedly both loud and dramatic, he'd quit and stormed from the office.

Tramping back through the rain back to the alley, Sean had found only a large wet concrete space and a few splinters of glass where his car had been. Having no cash for a bus or taxi he had walked home, cold and sodden, by which time the sky had grown dark to match his mood.

The fact that the garden gate refused to open must have seemed like the rancid cherry atop a particularly hideous cake and nobody reading of Sean's day could have blamed him for losing his temper. Pouring his fury into the inanimate object that was adding insult to injury, he had given the gate a brief but savage kicking.

There was no possible way for Sean to have known that, just under an hour earlier, two young men had broken into his home and viscously assaulted his wife before snatching a small amount of cash and some jewelry. It had been reported as a miracle that considering the significant injuries she had received, including a fractured skull, she had been able to drag herself as far as the garden gate before passing out.

Of course it was no consolation at all to Sean that his wife would almost certainly have died anyway or that, by inadvertently snapping her neck with his violent outburst towards the gate, he had in fact given her a mercifully quick death.

NINE STOP TRIP

It was a horrible story, somehow made even more real and distressing by the fact that it had happened to someone I knew, albeit vaguely. The world suddenly seemed a darker place than before, capable of horrors so much more real than those I saw on the TV every single night. I felt an urge to do something, anything, to help Sean, to make things better.

Being brutally honest with myself however I realised that not only was there nothing I could do but also that this urge was mainly inspired by my own desire to lift the dark cloud the story had cast over my world. In the weeks that followed I thought of Sean every so often and was saddened but, as time passed, that cloud became smaller and smaller.

A few months later I was making my way over to my favourite second hand bookshop, just strolling along in the burgeoning sunshine and not really thinking about anything. I passed the large cream coloured wall that was perpetually being graffitied and painted over. The latest temporary slogan staggered the full length on the wall in shaky, foot high letters and read:
"WALL! HUH! WHAT IS IT GOOD FOR?"

Chuckling to myself I passed by and glanced up the street I was about to cross just in time to see a young man stepping out on to the pavement, pulling his garden gate to behind him. The sound of that gate clattering closed triggered something in me and, in an instant, the warmth of the struggling sun lost its intensity and the humour of the wall went with it.

Lost in thought, or rather the avoidance thereof, I turned onto the familiar narrow back street and then again onto an increasingly leafy but always quiet residential road. On complete autopilot now I turned another corner, then another and found myself leaving tarmac to descend the usual little cobbled street.

The quite literally, underground bookshop and record store snuggled together behind the great graffiti murals that emblazed their backstreet frontages. Through the bright yellow door, down a couple of steps and I had arrived.

My favourite second hand bookshop was actually a bare stone cellar with a smooth cold floor and decaying roof. Somehow however, the floor to ceiling bookcases that filled every single wall managed to bring a unique warmth and cosiness to the place.

The owner was, as usual, in friendly conversation with a customer. Today it was an earnest and bearded young man with long dark hair and scruffy clothes, I'd seen him before but we'd never spoken. Seeing me the older man smiled, nodded and raised a welcoming hand. I returned the gesture before turning my attention to the myriad spines that surrounded me, each demanding my consideration in their own unique way.

Standing there, my head on my right shoulder as I scanned the shelves, I heard someone else pass through the door and down the steps but didn't really pay any attention. I was vaguely aware of some enquiry being made but still I focussed on the wealth of literature before me. I retrieved the odd volume here and there, breaking the old rule over and over.

In fact it wasn't until a voice, suddenly very close by, tentatively called my name that I straightened up and looked round.

"Anna?" Sean said, his face a shockingly gaunt question mark. For a moment I was too stunned to say anything, but as another second ticked by I managed to close my mouth and compose myself before replying.

"Hi," was the best I could manage initially, but managed to follow up quickly with, "it's been a while. D'you know I was just thinking about you." He seemed to relax a little, but only a little. He fidgeted with a slim volume he clasped with both hands, it was exceedingly well thumbed and haemorrhaging makeshift bookmarks.

"I thought it was you." He managed a weak smile, but this faltered as an uncomfortable silence elbowed its way into our corner of the shop. "But I wasn't sure," he added, before biting his bottom lip anxiously. We stood for a few moments more as I desperately tried to think of any possible subject for conversation, besides the obvious.

"Buying or selling?" I asked brightly, nodding at the book he held. Christ, I thought, even his hands look thin. A vague panic seemed to grip him while he looked at me blankly before staring down at the book. He seemed to gaze at it for just a little too long before bringing his eyes back to meet mine, comprehension finally putting in an appearance.

"Oh," he managed, "no. I just keep this with me. I've found it very helpful since..." his mouth hung open and an invisible wave seemed to crash over him. His eyes flickered and he rocked back on his heels a little, letting out a short gasp as he did so. In complete panic I ploughed on, desperate to maintain a 'normal' conversation.

"Seen anything you like?" my breezy, care free tone seemed out of place to the point of the ridiculous but it appeared to do the trick as he came back to me and responded.

"I was after some more Burroughs actually," he waved the battered paperback at me which I now recognised as being a copy of 'Naked Lunch' by the beat writer William Burroughs. It didn't strike me as a particularly uplifting title, let alone the kind of thing to help someone through what Sean had experienced, but then what did I know?

"I'd heard this chap had a first edition of The Soft Machine, y'know the next in the trilogy, but it turns out that guy with the beard beat me to it." He shrugged hopelessly and the awkward silence returned.

"Well, I should probably pay for these," I said, raising the books I was holding to underline my point. I made to walk to past him but found I couldn't just let it go.

"Look, Sean," I started, "I was really sorry to hear about, y'know, what happened." My free hand landed on his arm but he wouldn't hold my gaze.

NINE STOP TRIP

"Thanks," he almost whispered, staring intently at the bare stone floor. "I'm ok though," his head snapped up abruptly, his eyes suddenly brighter and meeting my own. "I've got my books." The smile he attempted was still weak, but now determined and I returned it.

"Take care of yourself yeah?" I said, stepping past him.

"Yeah, you too," I heard him say vaguely.

I paid for my books and left, glancing back over my shoulder as I did so. Sean was stood more or less as I'd left him apparently engrossed in a title he had found. I paused to look at the shell of a man I had known. Perfectly still, he was wide eyed with desperate focus on the text before him, his mouth hanging slightly ajar in unconscious yet reserved awe.

With a sad frown I turned and, shaking my head, stepped back out into the sun. Obviously the horrific events of a couple of months earlier had had scarred him deeply and, walking home, I hoped desperately that he would find a way through it all. Despite my surprise in his particular choice of subject matter, his literary pursuits seemed to be providing some kind of crutch and I felt glad he had that at least.

It was another couple of months before I ran into Sean again in a chance meeting that was as bizarre as it was brief. I'd walked through the park enjoying the birdsong and vibrant green on my way to the university. An artist I particularly liked was having an exhibition at the campus gallery and, finding myself with an afternoon to spare, I had decided to go along.

Making my way across campus I had noted various differences and similarities to my own time at university but tried not to dwell on how just long ago that had been. A figure in the crowd had drawn my attention from some distance as well as attracting glances from all sides.

What had caught my eye, and those of many other people it seemed, were the two vast hold alls the man was carrying. The broad black straps across each shoulder formed a startling X across his chest which was flanked by the great round bags on either side. This gave him the appearance, I noted with a smile, of a mobile game of noughts and crosses.

I was trying to find a pun relating sandwich boards to stock cubes and had almost walked past the man when I saw the bags were quite literally bursting with books. Various corners and seams had split or worn to reveal bland, contorted pages or the occasional flash of cover colour. Glancing from bag to bag to the man's face, I noticed he was looking right at me and then, finally, I realised it was Sean.

"Hey!" he said, his eyes wide and bright. He hadn't gained any weight, in fact if anything he looked even thinner, but something else had definitely changed. The palpable zeal and intensity that had dominated my first impression of him were back with a vengeance and I half expected to receive some kind of electric shock as he vigorously shook my hand.

We exchanged pleasantries while I scrutinised his face for any trace of the broken little boy I'd met at the bookshop. In the end I had to admit he seemed genuinely up and simply could not hold back any longer.

"So, you got enough books there or...?" I asked, nodding at the bags which must have weighed an absolute ton, though Sean didn't seem to mind.

"These?" he replied laughing, "I'm just taking them home, I got some really good stuff, hang on..." He began to rummage intently through the bag on his right.

"You bought all these today?" I asked, realising I was frowning.

"Here it is," he said, apparently ignoring my question while dragging a glossy paperback from the throng. "A great example of what I'm working with at the moment." He thrust the book at me expectantly.

"Oh you got a new job," I said, accepting the volume. "What are you doing?" The book was called 'Blood Electric' and had been written by someone called Kenji Siratori. I began to flick through as Sean talked.

"I'm kind of working outside the system at the moment..." I noticed that the format of 'Blood Electric' was not dissimilar to the Burroughs books Sean had been interested in the last time we'd met. This author however, had used various symbols among the familiar letters to give the feel of computer code to the text.

"...I'm involved in a project, early days as yet but just you wait..." I had heard this style referred to as 'cutup' due to its fragmented nature. Basically grammar and other traditional literary structures were abandoned in favour of a kind of free form poetry.

"...you could call it a communication experiment I suppose but ultimately it'll reach way beyond that..." Personally I'd always found this kind of thing frustratingly difficult to read. Friends of mine had tried to explain to me it as a kind of literary magic eye picture. Instead of focussing on each word in turn you had to just relax into it and let the words flow over you.

"...I'm really very excited about it, I can't say much at the moment but we're aiming to start production pretty soon..." It was about feeling the text rather than reading it, or so I'd been told. I handed the book back to Sean, feeling a great sense of relief as I did so. He seemed to be getting himself together and starting to move on. The world seemed a slightly better place once more.

"Great to see you again anyway," he said with a grin. "I'll let you know when..."

A great calming wave began ease over me as we stood in the glorious sunshine. If someone who'd been through something so horrifically tragic could bounce back then there was real hope for the rest of... Just then a muffled bellow shout broke into my reverie from some distance. I turned to see two men in security uniforms puffing their way towards us. I span back, questions already at my lips, but Sean was already off and making surprisingly good speed considering the load he carried.

While his receding figure was distinctly comedic, the slapstick guards huffing away after him only making it more so, I was left with a slight pang of concern. Despite the fact that he had seemed in much better place emotionally, I had wondered what he'd had to do to get there and just what he'd got himself into. I didn't find out that Sean had been stealing books from the university library until much later.

As a rule I don't tend to buy books new, I prefer both the character of second hand books, and the ambience of second hand book shops. A few months ago however I found myself in the city with some time to kill so I wandered into the local glossy outpost of a multinational bookselling chain to see what was what.

Doing my best to ignore the music and the crowds I focussed on the mammoth volume of stock, taking my time and gradually building a small pile of paperbacks under my arm. Having collected half a dozen potential purchases I rode the escalator to the top floor and approached the cafe area.

Secure in itself as an even greater commercial entity than its host, the coffee bar seemed content to nestle modestly towards the back of the upper floor. I had no intention of buying any coffee but, having checked my watch, was looking for somewhere comfortable to kill some more time and review my potential purchases.

Glancing about I noticed a table by the window flanked with two cosy looking armchairs, only one of which was occupied. Making my way between various other tables and patrons I approached the half taken table, considering the occupant who was apparently engrossed in his laptop computer.

I'd actually drawn breath to enquire if my desired seat was as free as it appeared before I recognised Sean. His hair was a little longer and, I noticed with some relief, he seemed to have put a little weight back on. He was dressed in casual but expensive looking clothes that, while appearing out of character to me, were entirely in keeping with the flashy computer equipment that was monopolising his attention.

"Sean?" My gentle opener went unnoticed, bouncing off a shell of intense concentration. "Sean," I said again, a little more firmly and with extra volume. This time I got through, though at first I almost wished I hadn't. Frowning, Sean tore his eyes away from the screen and glared up at me until recognition adjusted his features, but only slightly.

One eyebrow left its irritated huddle to arch in mild surprise while his eyes softened slightly from annoyance to cool calculation. Without a word he turned back to the laptop, tapped a few keys, and then appeared to read intently for a second or two, mumbling something incoherent. Finally he turned back to face me, only now wearing a broad expression of delighted surprise.

"Anna!" he exclaimed. "How great to see you, sit down, sit down," he stood as he gestured to the empty chair opposite him. For a moment I hesitated, wondering if I had actually imagined his briefly bizarre behaviour, but soon found myself settling into the leather upholstery and arranging my books on the table.

We settled into some fairly standard and pleasant small talk and the situation would have been downright everyday if not for Sean's apparent inability to leave his laptop alone. Every so often his left hand would drift over the keyboard and tap away, after which his eyes would scan over a few resultant lines which he would mouth to himself before returning to the world around him.

Eventually we began to run low on everyday banter and Sean's persistent division of attention began to irritate me. "So what's so interesting on there then?" I asked, nodding to the laptop.

"This?" he said, suddenly fully focussed and excited, an almost mischievous grin across his face, "this is the next step in our cultural evolution, in fact this is a revolution just waiting to happen!"

Now this isn't exactly a claim you come across every day but, as a writer, I like to think I can produce the right words for any situation.

"Really," I said, annoyed at my sudden

Adam Byfield

inability to find anything better.

"How much suffering, do you think, is caused by misunderstanding?" From being unable to hold Sean's attention for more than a few seconds at a time I now found myself under an intense and relentless gaze. I'd had enough of being on the back foot and so, giving myself a mental shake, I stepped up.

"Plenty I would think, in fact looking at socio-political problems across the board I'd say lack of empathy is a key, if not defining factor in most." Ha, have that.

Sean's palms bounced together in a sharp clap that caused me, and several other people to jump a little, before clenching into fists and shaking them about in celebration. "Exactly!" he beamed. "Empathy! That's the key, that's the word, excellent!" He was practically vibrating with enthusiasm.

"What would you say," he said in the lowered tones of giddy conspiracy, "if I told you that some of us have found a way to communicate feelings?" His eyes were unsettlingly wide but I tried to ignore the manic atmosphere he had created while I took in what he'd said.

"People do that all the time don't they?" I asked uncertainly. "Talking, body language, art, design, we've been doing it forever."

"Ah," Sean raised a finger and I was suddenly reminded of the pretension I had detected in him the first time we'd met. "You're right, there has always been communication of a sort, but it has never been complete, not until now!" I could feel myself openly frowning but Sean didn't seem to notice.

"You said it yourself," he continued with a smug grin that, in that moment, made me forget any compassion I had ever felt for him. "Empathy is what's missing. All we have now is sympathy. We get a vague idea of what someone else is going through but the best we can do is try to imagine how we would feel if we were in their place."

He paused to draw breath and I began to suspect I was witnessing a rehearsed speech. How many times have you said these words to yourself Sean, I wondered as he continued.

"What we're talking about here," he said, glancing at his laptop for the first time since embarking on his sermon, "is the ability to record a particular emotion, pass it to someone else and have them experience exactly what you felt. True understanding, genuine and complete!"

I don't know whether I appeared confused or just incredulous but after an awkward pause he decided further clarification was necessary.

"Ok look," he began, "I never had pets as a child, my father wouldn't allow them in the house, so I never knew how it felt to form an emotional bond with an animal. Now you have a dog don't you?"

"I did," I responded a little icily, "he died recently."

"Even better!" Sean's face actually lit up, not the reaction I had been expecting.

"Pardon?" I asked. There was open

irritation in my voice now but Sean didn't seem to notice and I didn't care.

"How can you convey to me how that must feel?" he ploughed on, practically giddy. I crossed my arms and shrugged, saying nothing.

"Until now you couldn't, those feelings were trapped in your head, you were at their mercy. But now..." he turned once more to his laptop, seemingly lost in admiration for whatever it displayed. After a moment's reverent silence he continued.

"Taking cut-up literature as a starting point we've developed a system whereby specific emotional states can be captured by certain combinations of words. Imagine how much better you'd feel if you could take feelings like your grief, and trap them on paper. They'd be there when you wanted them but you wouldn't be burdened by them when you didn't."

My mounting anger was suddenly checked by the realisation of why these crazy ideas might seem so appealing to Sean. It was no wonder he seemed so much happier now since our first encounter, he'd clearly used this project or whatever it was to escape from his guilt and grief rather than face them.

"Then, when you wanted somebody else to understand," he was saying, "they can just read it and then they'll feel exactly like you and they'll get it. It's amazing, a revolution like I said." Drawn back to his laptop he began to explain the specifics of his passion.

"We started with books you see," he

explained, "reading them and sharing particularly powerful passages online. We were trying to determine just what made them so powerful so that we could harness that power..."

"Who's we?" I interrupted.

"Well there're only a handful of us at the moment, scattered across the globe, but soon there'll be..." Seeing another prepared speech looming I butted in once more.

"The thing is Sean," I wasn't sure how to say it but I felt I had to try, "I don't think I want take those feelings out of my head." This stopped him dead, an abject lack of comprehension stalling his previously animated face. I could see a question forming on his pale lips but didn't give him chance to ask it.

"He was my dog," a pang of sadness snatched at my throat but I pushed past it, "and the connection we had was unique to the two of us. It makes me sad to think about him now but it also makes me happy as well, do you see?" The expression on his face told me he was struggling.

"I think I see what you're saying," Sean said quietly and eventually, and just for a moment I thought I saw a flash of that vacant terror that had almost overwhelmed him in the bookshop. I suddenly found myself feeling incredibly guilty, after all who was I to say that the way he was choosing to deal with his wife's appalling death was wrong?

"Look, Sean..." I began but he cut me off, his former vigour returned only now with a more serious edge.

"It's an interesting point Anna, thanks; I'll mention it to the others." Listlessly he tapped at the laptop's keyboard before seeming to shake himself. "Anyway if you'll excuse me I'm actually rather busy."

"Sure, of course," I said, gathering up my books and standing. "Look after yourself Sean yeah?"

He nodded vaguely in my direction before focussing back on the glowing screen. As I made my way back to the escalators I found I was no longer in the mood for either reading or browsing. Beginning my descent I glanced back at the man by the window. He hadn't moved and, in that moment, didn't look like he ever would again.

My train got in just after lunch, I'd been away for just under a week. Feeling refreshed by the trip and energised by the violently blue sky overhead, I decided not to join the taxi queue but to walk home instead.

The familiar city streets seemed unusually vibrant in the summer sun as I made my way up and through, eventually leaving the shops and the throng behind. Cutting across the university campus I soon found myself entering the park, I was almost home.

Knots of people were scattered across the great swathes of green, the odd dog or football flitting in between. The air was thick with relaxed and happy sounds, as if the afternoon would last forever and I slowed to a stroll to soak up the feeling.

Whichever way I looked I saw smiles, that is until a figure on the path up ahead caught my eye. Even shielding my eyes, all I could make out was a person wearing a heavy looking ankle length coat standing in the shade of the trees that flanked the park's tarmac spine. I continued making my way through the park but now found my attention irritatingly centred on the mysterious figure ahead.

It wasn't until I was just a few feet away that I recognised the man in the long coat. I suppose I should have guessed really but it'd been quite a while since I'd seen Sean with his laptop and, I suppose partly because he'd seemed to be doing well financially, I hadn't really worried about him too much since.

Now however, here he was, standing in front of me, in the middle of summer, wearing a huge winter coat and cursing a group of teenagers stood a little further on. I was pretty sure that if I kept walking he wouldn't even notice me but he looked about ready to drop, probably from the heat.

"Cold eyes ... fast legs ... buzzing all time ... but I am not a cow," he was saying, only vaguely to the jeering youngsters. I went to take a step toward him but stalled when... "I have no tail!" he roared at them, throwing his hands up in the air. I noticed he was holding something.

The youths whooped and crowed, clearly enjoying the show. Sean returned to muttering, apparently without sense but guardedly fell silent and stuffed whatever he had into a deep pocket as I stepped up to him and said hello. Wet, vacant eyes flickered loosely over my face, only to be narrowed a moment later by a frown.

Unsure how to proceed I watched as he began to rifle through his huge, filthy coat. I noticed his hands were dirty, his nails black, as he searched through what appeared to be dozens of homemade pockets stitched into the lining of the coat.

A couple of times he paused to remove a sheaf of greasy looking paper scraps from a pocket, before muttering to himself in irritation and continuing his search. Finally he found the bundle he was looking for and straightened up to face me.

Absently licking a grubby thumb he leafed through what I realised was a homemade book, basically shopping receipts and corners of newspapers and stained napkins, all scribbled on and bound together with a tangle of wire and string.

"Balloon burst at the funeral, he is behind them, not dead!" Sean nodded the words to me through a broad, and slightly manic smile. His eyes were painfully hopeful, apparently expecting me to grasp his meaning. After a few seconds had gone by his bright expression faltered and he grimaced, returning to his book.

"Surprise," he said slowly, as if speaking to a child, "confusion, and joy!" with this last his eyes lit up. I smiled and felt myself nodding, I thought maybe I understood.

NINE STOP TRIP

"It's good to see you too?" I ventured, this seemed to please him. "So, I haven't seen you in a while, how've you been?" It seemed ridiculous but what else could I say?

Raising a finger inviting me to wait, Sean quickly swapped the book he held for another and I realised this was what I had seen him holding just minutes before. Again we stood in silence, surrounded by the hubbub of the busy park and an occasional flash of apathetic spite from the kids.

I began to glance around at the other, joyously sunlit world that lay just a few feet away. Because of this I didn't see the young boy creep up behind Sean but turned back just in time to see him snatch Sean's book from his hand and rush back toward his friends.

Screaming an awful, inhuman sound, Sean set off after the boy, his coat flailing out behind him. The teenagers fled the park with Sean tumbling desperately after them. I was alone in the shade. Walking the rest of the way home I was reminded of that day in the bookshop, all those months ago. The day, as busy and beautiful as it was, had again somehow lost its sheen to me.

Getting in I couldn't leave thoughts of Sean behind, he'd run so far from his grief he now seemed to be hopelessly lost, though I hoped desperately to be wrong. Finding myself unable to focus on any of the various tasks I had planned I came up here to write this. Somehow putting things down on paper always seem to help.

Adam Byfield

PILE UP
PILE UP
PILE UP
PILE UP
PILE UP

The street is long, dark and increasingly wet. Within the familiar winter evening, houses huddle in on themselves in two neat rows flanking the road. Occasionally broken lines of silent cars run the length of both kerbs and the drizzle gets just a little bit heavier.

The cold bites from the air and creeps through the rain, seeking to chill everything to its own frigid level. The hallmarks of life abound in the shadows and yet nothing will move, breathe or shine. The street is empty, dead, with neither animal nor person just...

...wait.

That car there, not the first one you noticed but the third or the fourth, yes that one. Isn't there a shape there? Behind the wheel, a deeper shadow, a figure, a man? The car is as mediocre, as normal, as nondescript as could be imagined. Nothing about it draws even the slightest attention, except for the man at wheel.

The drizzle is collecting evenly across the rear window, occasionally erupting into heavy droplets that plunge gleefully downward. The back seat of the car is clean and clear and, despite it's obvious age, the car's interior smells fresh and new.

There is no movement nor sound in the car, just the constant, subtle drumming of the rain against the roof. The figure in the driver's seat sits motionless but, in time, you realise you can just about hear him breathing. At this point you notice something hanging from rear view mirror, a small object strung on a thread.

To your surprise the object is familiar. While to most people such a thing would be so mundane as to be invisible, for you it has profound significance. A personal secret, an everyday treasure, a talisman of value only to you.

Somehow you find the presence of this object upsetting. Not only has this man stolen the uniqueness of your charm, but he has destroyed its sacred secret nature by advertising its significance for all to see. You follow the thread up and away from your defiled icon towards the...

...eyes in the mirror above!

The man alone in his car turns abruptly, running wide eyes over his back seat so clean and clear. He drives his gaze frantically around the empty space in the car, his knuckles whitening on the seats.

"My god," he whispers, "you're here."

He continues to stare into the dark empty spaces, even peering out through each window in turn. The sound of his body moving against the upholstery seems to roar through the still night. Eventually however, he settles back into his original, stonelike pose. For a few minutes once more, there is only the sound of the rain.

Adam Byfield

"I knew you'd come."

His whisper comes suddenly, without motion, almost as if the words are condensing from the chilled air within the car. "I've waited here for so very long," he continues, "time without measure. Sometimes I thought..." but, apparently overcome by emotion, he stops here.

For a while longer you both listen to the rain. When he finally speaks again his voice is calmer, more measured and yet somehow more intense. "So this is it," he hisses, "I finally get to do it all, to *feel* it all. It's started already hasn't it? Yes, I can tell." His breathing has become more audible.

"Ok, ok," he shifts his weight in the driver's seat, "I'm ready. This is how it began..."

It is a glorious summer day, everyone and everything seems vibrant and overflowing with life. You suspect that the interior of the cafe would normally appear dingy, but on a day like today, with a great golden wall of sunlight piling in through the windows, it seems bright and airy.

Despite the bustling street outside, you count only three people in here. A young and slender girl sits behind the counter, leaning forward to rest her chin in her hand. You can't quite make out the title of the book she is reading.

Towards the back of the cafe you see the man from the car. Here you can see him fully and in detail, yet you are disappointed. Below his severely cut, dull brown hair, you find his face to be as nondescript as his vehicle. You run your eyes all over his oblivious form, filling in the shadows you remember from the car. The only words you can find however, are *ordinary* and *normal*, you're even tempted towards *boring*.

Medium height and build, he is sat quietly, staring across the empty tables towards the window. Occasionally he takes a sip from the cup of tea sat alone on the table before him. You look back to the girl and note that they both appear not to notice the only sound in the place. Your eyes are now drawn to the much taller man sat eating between the two of them.

Beneath this table two long and muscular legs extend from a pair of fashionably cut shorts. The expensive looking polo shirt he wears is just tight enough to relay the various contours of his upper body. As you watch he piles another forkfull of food into his already full mouth. You can see his mouth is full because he holds it open as he chews.

The sounds of his cutlery grinding against his plate periodically punctuates the constant sticky slopping sound of his enthusiastic jaw. Leaning in to receive another fried load, the man turns his head to look at the girl behind the counter. Chomping heartily he stares at her for a while, you get the impression he is thinking.

"What's the book?" he calls hoarsely, spraying tiny pieces of wet food into the air to catch the light. You see her eyes stop reading and her lips tighten slightly before she tilts the book to reveal the cover. It is one you know, not the last book you read, but the one before that. She has a different edition with a more colourful cover, but you recognise the title and author's name.

"You don't want to read that," he continues, pausing only to swallow, "it's shite. Why don't you come and sit over here?"

You look back to the girl just in time to see her frown fade as she returns to the book. Suddenly the atmosphere feels heavy with more than just humidity. Looking back you notice the knife and fork still in his hands but no longer moving.

"Oi," his tone is lower now, "I'm fucking talking to you."

The girls eyes flick from her book to the man, now glaring at her, and then briefly over his shoulder before returning to the text. You realise she has made eye contact with the man from the car, who has now finished his tea and has turned in his chair.

Very slowly the man in the middle leans his cutlery against the edge of his plate before abruptly slamming both palms down on the table. You, his cutlery, his plate and the girl, all jump at this sudden explosion of noise.

She drops her book but scrabbles to retrieve it and act as if nothing has happened. The man chuckles spitefully, his palms still flat on the table, his eyes boring into her. Suddenly you notice that the man from the car is on his feet, he's at the other man's table.

Tearing his eyes from the girl, the seated man looks up at the stranger beside him. Before he can voice the question on his brow however, the man from the car has acted. It happens so quickly and yet, afterward, you remember it in slow motion.

In one smooth, arcing movement the ordinary, normal, boring man scoops up both knife and fork and brings them back down into the backs of the seated man's hands. One impact comes hot the heels of the first and makes the whole thing sound like a musical punchline.

Unable to look away you watch as the seated man looks from his hands, now both pinned to the table and starting to bleed, up into the bland face of his attacker. A moment more and he looks back to his hands. Now he begins to scream.

The man from the car turns to the girl, with a huge grin on his face you notice. The girl is on her feet now and has dropped her book onto the counter. Her eyes are wide and glassy and her bottom lip trembles below an open mouth.

Just for a second you're sure you see a flicker of doubt and confusion ripple through the wide grin she is faced with. After this however, the man from the car lets out a deep and satisfied sigh, his enthusiastic grin settling back into an expression of such comfortable pleasure.

For what seems like ages you watch the unchanging scene: the girl's head bobbling slightly atop her slender neck; the man from the car just standing there watching and apparently loving it; while all the time the other man thrashes and squeals in the background. You are transfixed by the figures, the emotions until, suddenly, the man from the car turns on his heel and steps out into the blinding light.

"That was amazing," he says, his elbow resting against the door, his hand on the steering wheel. Still the rain comes, playing it's scattered rhythm across the car roof above. "I mean that was just, so fucking good." He shakes his head, apparently in wonder.

"The thing about that was..." he begins but breaks off, sliding down in his seat as far as he can before freezing absolutely still. For a few seconds nothing happens and you are utterly confused by his actions, but now there are voices and footsteps.

A few seconds more and a couple hurry past, clinging together, heads down, eager to reach somewhere warm and dry. Their footsteps and chatter fade as you watch their forms blend into the murk further up the street.

Slowly the man works his way back in to a sitting position and checks carefully out of all the windows before speaking again. You notice his tone is more hushed than before. "The thing about that was I thought she'd be pleased."

At first this sentence seems abstract and meaningless but then you realise he's referring to the cafe. "When she first looked at me we had this, moment, you know? We were both thinking the same thing, and we both knew we were both thinking it, you get me?" Again he shakes his head.

"Yeah, it was great. I'd never felt a connection like that with anyone before, it made me feel real, like I was really alive." His hushed tones are only just managing to contain his enthusiasm. "As soon as he put his cutlery down I knew what I was going to do, I mean what a prick." He laughs quietly.

"But anyway," he recovers himself and continues, "I really thought she'd be pleased. I thought she be glad to see him get it and grateful to me for sorting it." He frowns gently, it seems to you he's struggling to recapture his feelings of the time.

"So I did it, I mean you saw me do it, and there she is, fucking terrified." He shifts in his seat apparently not yet as comfortable as he had been earlier. "The thing was..." he seems reluctant and yet at the same time eager to say it, "that felt even better."

"Her being scared of me, that's when I felt really real. Fuck the connection, fuck thinking the same thing, in that moment I changed everything about her, I fucking defined her. Me." He closes his eyes, revelling in the memory. You feel awkward and uncomfortable but outside the car is only darkness and rain.

"I got such a buzz from it," he's back and there's more. "It lasted days, I didn't think there could be anything better," he laughs, "how wrong was I?" He finally seems to have settled and has returned to his motionless stance, giving his voice a slightly disturbing disembodied quality.

Adam Byfield

"No, I was on the bus, not long after that, and these two young girls got on and sat in front of me. I wasn't really paying any attention at first but then I realised what they were talking about. They were telling the story of that day!

"Total strangers! Talking about me, about what I'd done. I realised that just that one little thing had made me real to people I'd never even met! That was it, that was when I knew, I had to do something else, something that would get people talking..."

It is one of the those late summer evenings where the sky pretends its earlier than it is, but the chill in the air reminds you that it's not. The young man is walking uphill carrying a backpack and a weary but satisfied expression on his face.

Looking at his clothes and watching him cross the road, you decide he is a college student, finally on his way home after a day of lessons and an evening of study. Everything is grey in the dying sunlight but as he makes his way down that flight of stairs, dropping away from you and the pavement, you see the gaudy yellow of the subway come into view.

There's no-one else around and the only sounds are the traffic on the dual carriageway above and the young man's footsteps. You notice the change in these footsteps as he enters the subway, the enclosed space lends them an echoing depth lost on the street above.

He's halfway through the bright yellow

tunnel, glancing at the graffiti on either wall. His skin appears strange and sickly in the artificial light and as he clears his throat you get the sense something is wrong. He's approaching the far end of the subway, he's nearly there. You relax a little as you watch him step out into the fresh air and darkness, he's...

...being dragged back in to the tunnel!

A darkly dressed figure has appeared from the blackness beyond and is now grappling with him! They fall against a particularly colourful patch of wall and you see the young man's assailant raise his hands.

Before you can think you hear the young man's head connect sickeningly with the wall. You hear a groan as he sinks to the floor and notice a downward growing dark patch amidst the picture he leaves behind.

Closer now and, as you suspected, you recognise the dark clad figure. The man from the car is hauling his victim to his knees. Dazed but not quite out, the young man bats drunkenly at the hands closing about his throat.

As pressure is applied you see both men begin a gradual build of emotion. Somewhere within the young man on his knees synapses are firing and adrenalin is being released. You can see clarity fading back into his eyes, now they're widening as he finally catches up with the situation.

He is fighting hard but the man from the car is also changing. His silence has been broken by increasingly ragged breath. You look at his face and are shocked to find him baring his teeth in a leering grimace.

The man on his knees is rasping something but you can't make it out. You watch as he claws at the hands about his throat and tries to push himself up from the floor. The man from the car leans into his task though, grunting with the exertion. Spittle falls from his animal maw into the desperate face below.

Trying to blink the fluid away, the younger man is making the strangest and most terrible sound you've ever heard from a real person, but still it goes on. The images threaten to overwhelm you: yellow light sickly skin bulging eyes bared teeth grunts and rasping moans, your head begins to spin...

...and it is done.

The man from the car staggers back to lean against the opposite wall, his breath tearing in and out of him, the sound filling the subway. The younger man tumbles forward, his vacant face striking the stone floor with a sound that causes you to wince even though you know he can't feel it.

Everything seems somehow colder and more distant now. The dark shapes in the yellow light are somehow flatter and duller. You feel numb as you watch the man from the car manhandle the corpse he has created. He drags what was, until just moments before, an innocent young man, to the very centre of the subway.

You observe without comprehension as he positions the limbs just so, bent at strange angles to form a terrible shape on the floor. The man from the car disappears off into the far darkness and you are left alone with the body.

With some difficulty you manage to pry your eyes away and force yourself to concentrate on the graffiti instead. It looks just like the graffiti you sometimes see at home but your brain simply cannot ignore what is lurking in the corner of your eye.

Thankfully a sound enters the subway to offer some distraction. It is the man from the car, he has returned and is carrying a traffic cone and a couple of kitchen utensils. As you watch him gently place the cone over the young man's discoloured face and oh so carefully fit the utensils into stiffening fingers, you desperately look for some sense, some reason.

You find none. Stepping back to admire his work, the man from the car, to your disgust, actually rubs his hands together before turning and walking back in to the dark. You wait for a while, but this time he does not come back.

There is sound and motion outside. The front door of the house closest to the car has opened and silhouetted in the glowing doorway is a woman with two young children. She's herding them out of the door and pushing some suitcases in the same direction with her feet.

You can just about make out the children's complaints as they stand in the rain waiting for their mother to snap off the light and lock the door.

Taking a case in each hand she shoos the children towards the kerb, following close behind.

You realise that the man in the driver's seat is hunched down low again, but not as far as before. He watches with interest as the woman unlocks the car parked just in front of this one and bundles the kids and cases into it. She seems in quite a rush and moments later you hear the engine rumble and watch as the car pulls away into the night.

The man in the front stares on until the car is nothing but a pair of hovering lights. As those lights wink out into the distance he gets comfortable in his seat once more and begins to speak. "Yeah," he says quietly, "that thing in the subway was pretty intense."

He quickly runs a hand over his face and head before pulling absently at his neck. "I don't know really," he continues, "the act itself wasn't supposed to be anything for me, just some messed up shit that people would be sure to talk about."

The rain is heavier now and adds pressure to the silence that follows.

"Worked though," he says finally in a brighter tone. "Everywhere I went, on the bus, in pubs, on the street; everywhere I turned there were people talking about it, talking about me. It felt good. It felt worth it. I really felt like I'd achieved something." You recoil at how calm and truthful he sounds here.

"The best bit though," he says, excitement creeping back into his voice, "was the papers.

NINE STOP TRIP

That had never even occurred to me but it was all over the front pages. I mean it's one thing to have people talking about you, but people are always talking about something and after a few weeks or months, whatever, they'll start to forget.

"The papers though," he bites his bottom lip, nodding to himself, "now that's really real. That's like recorded for all time, so it'll always be there. Like way, way in the future people will be able to read about that and I'll still be real even then."

Looking at him, slouched in the dark, you can't help but think of the images from the cafe and the sounds from the subway. You hope so dearly that he is satisfied, but you know he is not, he can't be. You know this isn't where the story ends, you know there is more to come, and sure enough...

"I realised then you see, that I needed something bigger, something truly great. If I wanted to be really, *really* real I needed something that could never be forgotten, something they'd be writing about forever..."

A museum at night can be an eerie place to be and this one is no exception. All around you strange, alien shapes lurk in the darkness. Everything is perfectly still and there is an utter absence of sound. It's a strange feeling to be in a public building after hours. Wide corridors built to accommodate crowds seem vast and menacing now.

You're reminded of a dream you had as a child, that one where you were at school but it was the middle of the night and you were alone. Your remembering is interrupted however, as the hairs on the back of your neck tell you you're about to hear something.

A few strained seconds pass until, there, just there, footsteps!

You find the high ceilings and hard floors make it difficult to work out where the sound is coming from, but you're sure it's getting closer. Slow, deliberate footfalls echo maddeningly around you as you look back and forth from one end of the corridor to another. Just where is that coming...

...light!

A torch beam leaps into view, it's circular touch slipping and sliding over walls and floor. Here and there tiny fragments of the exhibits are illuminated, flashes of texture and colour. The narrow, glowing column seems to run off into the darkness forever until a uniformed guard finally rounds the corner off to your left.

For an instant you are dazzled by the torch as the beam swings to face you head on. The guard keeps walking however, making his way down the empty corridor with practised ease. Closer now, you notice the shape of his hat and hear a muffled jingle of keys.

Reaching the far end of the corridor, you watch the guard turn lazily to head off along the next leg of his tour. He begins to whistle tunelessly as the shapes he leaves behind are consigned to the darkness once more. Except for that one, that shape there, the one that's moving!

The horrific scene in the subway flashes back into your mind and for a moment is superimposed over this one. The same black clad figure, emerging again as if from nowhere, lunges toward the guard from behind. The briefest of protests is almost instantly muffled as their forms merge in the darkness. You see the torch beam flailing wildly, tearing silently from floor to ceiling and back.

You find yourself frustrated that you cannot see what is happening and begin to move in closer, but then you remember the subway again and are thankful for the lack of the light. All you can hear are shoes scuffing against the floor and grunts of physical exertion.

What was that?

There was a flash, a glint of metal, just for an instant. Now another sound joins the shoes and replaces the grunts, you don't recognise it at first. A strange gurgling, a kind of desperate rasping gargle, followed by a thick dripping sound.

Your mind reels as it pictures the horrors that may lay in the darkness before you. You can just about make out one of the forms now slumping heavily to the polished floor. The torch finally comes to rest, it's beam now framing a uniformed leg and spastically twitching shoe.

For second after second the shoes dances on, clicking horribly against the floor. As it slows to a halt you realise you can hear breathing; familiar, ragged breathing. An abrupt squeal and slap makes you jump as the black clad figure steps forward and slips in something on the floor, almost but not quite falling.

You hear some more shuffling and another grunt as the torch suddenly slides off a few feet. A brief pause and it moves again. As the body, and the torch it still clings to, is dragged round the corner and away, your thoughts turn nauseously to a traffic cone and two kitchen utensils. You turn away from the site of the unseen scene and try to ignore the fading sounds of hard work except...

...there are people everywhere!

Sunlight is streaming in through the tall windows and the corridor is full of smartly dressed people. They are all chattering and moving in the same direction, utterly ignoring the exhibits, all now clearly visible and somehow less interesting for it. You realise that hours have passed in a heartbeat and, trying to get past your the feelings of disorientation, you start to follow the snaking crowd.

Round that same terrible corner and out into a vast and majestic space they file. Quite enormous paintings dominate the panelled walls while small glass cases are dotted about the gleaming patterned floor. Beneath and about these are yet more people, all dressed as if for a formal dinner and mostly sipping at slender glasses of sparkling wine.

At the heart of the room squats a huge, broad podium. The treasure it supports however is hidden from view by vast lengths of deep red material. Looking up, you see that the heavy folds run almost all the way to the ceiling where they are suspended from some complicated looking rigging.

Threading their way back and forth through the crowd you spy a few bored looking, young men and women. They carry metal trays, crystal glasses and plastic smiles. Towards the far side of the room another figure catches your eye. Deep in conversation with a particularly dapper looking couple is a man with a heavy beard. The glossy hair falling about his shoulders shifts as he laughs loudly along with the couple at the joke he has apparently just told.

This man definitely looks familiar but, right now, you can't quite place him. Before you can rack your brains sufficiently however a plump man in an immaculate suit and eye watering waistcoat approaches the room's grand, mysterious centrepiece.

Gradually the deafening chatter breaks down and soon all eyes are on the fat man as he begins his speech. You don't really pay attention to what's being said, scouring the crowd instead for the bearded man you noticed before.

You're vaguely aware of the man at the front thanking everyone for being there, something about the legendary throne of an ancient king, a once in a lifetime opportunity. The other man must have left as you can't seem to find him anywhere.

Movement draws your eyes back to the main event. Photographers are gathering in front of the speaker as he introduces some local dignitary or other. As the latter makes his formal address, his hand on a dramatic looking lever, you cast a final glance over your shoulder, but you still don't...

...no wait, there. There he is, grinning like crazy.

A bad feeling begins to twitch in the pit of your stomach as your turn back just in time to see the lever pulled. The acres of plush red are tumbling down, seeming to snub gravity's uncouth urgency in their grace. The deep rippling sound they make as they fall into broad, gentle folds on the floor runs right through you; it feels nice.

The crowd holds it breath, you hold your breath, as the last of the red sweeps down and down. With a fantastic flop sound the curtain is down, the magical treasure revealed. You can see the great bejewelled throne: it's huge glittering back standing tall; it's elephantine arms stamping down into the floor, but you're not looking at any of this.

Just like everyone else in the now deathly silent room, your eyes are locked on the inhumanly pale face of the uniformed corpse sat before you. Back straight, he wears an dark and unruly bib that runs from his ragged throat down over his crisp white shirt and looks distinctly sticky. His dull eyes stare back at the crowd and, for about half a second the stunned silence holds.

Now there is chaos, screams and stampeding. The plump man is red faced and wild eyed. He roars at two nearby waiters to help him as he tugs helplessly at a neatly folded stack of too heavy fabric. Your head begins to spin, everything is bodies and noise.

The doors to the room are suddenly too small as everyone tries to pass through them at once. Surveying the madness you catch a final glimpse of the bearded man, still grinning, before he is swept away on the frantic tide and disappears into the throng.

There is a disco in the car.

Blue slides rapidly over everything again and again as the police car cruises past. There is no siren but as they pass you see the officers within scrutinising each parked car in turn. They're clearly looking for someone and you're willing to bet it's the man in the front of you who has managed to fit almost his entire body into the driver's footwell.

You watch as the now full blown rain pelting the rear window distorts the retreating blue flashes. The man in the front stays in his cramped hiding place for what seems like a long time before finally easing back up into his seat. You notice he is smiling.

"Now I don't want blow my own trumpet," he begins, in hushed tones now familiar to you, "but that was fucking brilliant. I mean did you see their faces?" A silent wheezing laugh spills forth and you watch in revulsion as he doubles up in hysterics.

Finally he wipes a tear from his eye and sighs happily. "You wouldn't believe how itchy that wig was, I tell you, but it was so worth it." The grin he now wears is horribly familiar.

"I was walking home after that, I mean I felt ten feet tall, and all I could think about were the next day's papers, man, I couldn't wait. Anyway, I was so wrapped up in thinking about them that I almost walked straight passed the shop."

The sound of the rain on the roof is louder now, you can only just make out what is being said.

"There were all these TVs, different sizes, stacked up, all showing the museum. As I stood there watching, reading the little scrolly things across the bottom of the screens, that's when it came to me. Television man, if I could do someone live on TV, that would have to go global. The whole human race would know about it! How real would that make me?

"I really thought I'd worked it out then, you know. I mean by this point I knew could do anything, whatever I wanted, but I still didn't understand *why*. Oh, and that sour faced copper, Detective Inspector something or other, who came on later, vowing to *'bring me to justice'*," he sniggers, shaking his head. "That just made it even better, I mean if I'd only known then..."

He pauses, frowning.

"But we're not up to that yet, I'm getting ahead of myself. We have to do this in order or it won't work. No, at this point I thought TV was the pinnacle, I thought this would be my grand finale..."

NINE STOP TRIP

It's a bright, clear autumn morning. The cold makes the air seem clean and you relish the refreshing bite in the breeze as you survey the large crowd before you. Taking up most of the sizeable park, not unlike that one you visited a few years back, the crowd consists mostly of giddy teens, all focussed intently on the stage ahead.

Past the various cameras, under the complex looking lighting rigs and within the cables and scaffolding of the stage you can see the two twenty something presenters. You watch as they deliver their own brand of well practiced spontaneity to the enthusiastic crowd.

While you don't recognise these two specifically it occurs to you that they're pretty much interchangeable with various other bright young things you've seen on TV. Set back behind the stage, and off to one side, you notice a few vehicles huddling together. One of them, a large white van, supports a huge antenna that reaches up toward the clear sky, firing a constant but invisible stream of sound and picture.

A sudden increase in volume draws your attention back to the crowd. You realise that the presenters have asked for volunteers, hence the eager arms currently flailing above the sea of young faces. Eventually one boy and one girl, both in their late teens are selected from towards the front of the crowd and invited to make their way to the stage.

Seconds tick by as the two thread their way through the tightly packed crowd before finally being ushered on stage by a serious looking woman wearing headphones. Both lean in to the presenter's microphones to give their names, underlined by cheers and applause from their peers at their feet.

The video screen that dominates the rear of the stage melts from ambient backdrop into footage of the holiday the lucky two are about to play for. The crowd quietens during this display only to erupt back into whooping appreciation as the short film finishes and attention shifts back to the stage.

You watch with an occasional smile but increasing boredom as the head to head quiz progresses. When their contestants struggle both hosts give them outrageous clues, much to the delight of the crowd, to drive the whole thing to dramatic tie break situation.

With the tension built to an apparently sufficient level the final question is asked. To your surprise you don't actually know the answer but neither, it seems, does the boy who rushes to speak first. The pressure is now on as all eyes focus on the girl.

Her face appears on the screen behind her, so that the bottom lip she bites nervously is several feet wide. Just as you see the intense concentration begin to lift from her face however she suddenly frowns, raising her left arm slightly and looking down at her side, she moves to...

...fire!

There is no girl standing on the stage ahead of you now, just a twisting column of hungry flames amid three stunned statues. A terrible,

terrible scream is quickly drowned out as the crowd takes up the panicked refrain.

The stampede that follows is familiar to you now, not a single person hearing the broken voice of the male presenter as he pleads into his microphone for everyone to stay calm. From somewhere another man has appeared on stage with a fire extinguisher and is desperately dousing the flaming heap that has collapsed front and centre.

You see the other contestant, eyes goggling, being led away but then, finally, you turn away, not wanting to see anymore. The crowd is oozing away across the park and you can just make out the faint sound of sirens. That's when you notice the smell, oh god, the smell, it's...

...gone.

You're in a kitchen, small and bare. You overcome the annoyance of yet more disorientation by looking about you. A quick glance from the window tells you you're in a flat, several stories up. Trying to drown the hideousness of seconds earlier in new details, you ask yourself what is wrong with this picture.

It takes a little while but finally the flash of inspiration comes. The kitchen is empty, all surfaces perfectly clean and clear. You're reminded of those show kitchens you've seen in the huge DIY stores. All the trappings of home but lifeless, no identity, no soul.

You're reminded of something, of somewhere, another environment that felt like this. Before you can place it however, you hear a door open and close in the next room. Heavy breathing and hurried footsteps are cut short by the tinny sounds of a television.

Moving through the open doorway you are presented with another catalogue room. Full of furniture yet somehow empty, the television provides the only sound and motion. You can't quite make out the screen, obscured as it is by a large armchair, but you recognise the questions you can hear being asked and answered.

Sure enough, as you move sideways and the screen comes into view, the same two presenters are quizzing the same two kids. You feel a sense of dread at what you know is about to happen but are prevented from dwelling on it as the armchair's occupant moves onto his knees before the TV.

He fumbles for a moment with a videotape, cursing as he encourages it to enter the VCR that squats below the TV. The tape finally in, and a red light flashing on the VCR's display, the man drops back into his chair.

You can't help but watch as the terrible moment approaches, just before it arrives however your attention is somehow drawn away from the screen by a tiny *click* sound. Looking back you just catch a glimpse of the flames and the horror before the screen snaps to black.

The black is quickly replaced by the channel's logo and you can just make out a continuity announcer saying something about technical problems. It's hard to hear however, over the howling laughter from the man in the chair.

NINE STOP TRIP

You don't have to look, you know who he is. As he slaps his thigh and continues to roar something falls to the floor just in front of you. A small plastic box, utterly plain and smooth but for a simple red button. Involuntary questions begin to crowd into your head as the laughter goes on and on and on...

...and on.

The car rocks slightly as he shifts his weight and catches his breath. "Hoo," he sighs happily, "that was my proudest moment, it took me weeks to come down from that."

The rain is really coming down now, reducing visibility to just few feet around the vehicle. You can just about make out the looming mass of the nearest and recently vacated house, but that's about it. This evening of unanswered questions and horrible stories seems to be dragging pointlessly on, the rain just getting heavier, the night darker and colder. You realise the man up front has been speaking.

"Hey," he says, "thought I'd lost you for a moment there, don't do that to me yeah?" He seems genuinely rattled by something and you find, on some level at least, that this pleases you.

"That was a real test that one," he returns to his story. "Like I said before, I'd come to believe I could do as I pleased but I don't mind telling you, when it came down to it, I had some doubts. I slipped that thing in the girl's pocket as she made her way to the stage and then had to leg it all the way home.

"Part of me knew I couldn't go wrong but that didn't stop me praying as I ran back to the flat. Then I got in and turned the telly on, waited for the that golden moment, pressed the button and whoompf, up she went." He gives the moment to the rain and you can see him reliving it all over again.

"It's not the same," he says, apparently to himself, coming out of his reverie. "So anyway, I thought I'd made it you know, I thought I was finally there. That feeling of..." he breaks off again, with some effort this time you notice. "No," he continues, "we don't do this yet do we? No, it's this guy next."

You look around, out into the icy sheets of dark that hem you in. There is no-one around and the man's cryptic nonsense is becoming increasingly irritating. "He was all over the news," he continues, as if by way of explanation, "talking as if he knew all about me, goading me. Basically he didn't have a clue, he was trying to force my hand, trying to push me into a making a move so he could catch me and be the hero."

His tone is one of genuine pity for, you assume, the detective inspector he mentioned earlier.

"And so here we are..." his head snaps up, you can see his spine stiffening before you, "...and here we go!" As he leans forward and scrabbles for something under his seat, you peer through the shifting windscreen, alive with water, and try to make out what he has seen.

NINE STOP TRIP

By the time you make out the figure, head down, collar up, striding quickly toward the nearest house, the man in front is poised. He has snatched that special object from the mirror and now has one hand on the door handle while the other lies out of sight but apparently holds something important.

Out of the car and the rain is everything, beating all objects and even the air itself down into the slick ground. From somewhere far away you feel a vague echo of irrational fear that the rain will simply fill the world and drown you all, but more immediate events demand your attention.

The man on the street is just a couple of steps from his front door now, as you see the man from the car heading straight for him. Starting from a crouch, closing the car door silently, he gradually straightens up as he makes a bee line for the unsuspecting resident.

As he undergoes this strange evolution you notice, for the first time, that he is wearing the same all black outfit you've become uncomfortably familiar with. You watch as he times his run perfectly so that, just as the man opens the door, he is on him.

The single fluid motion from kerb to doorstep culminates in an arcing swing of the object you saw him retrieve from under his seat. The fleeting glimmer of metal takes you back to the museum but this time there is enough light for you to see the machete in its entirety.

You're already cringing but are still taken by surprise when the blade sweeps down and down only to bite into the backs of two innocent knees. The whole thing takes less than a second, tendons cut, keys dropped, bundled in, door slammed.

You're out in the rain. The house is dark. It's as if it didn't happen.

Inside however you can't escape the truth. Blood has already dyed most of the man's trousers, not to mention his hall carpet but the man from the car doesn't seem to notice. He stands astride the moaning figure, drops his machete and manhandles him onto his back. A black clad, and surprisingly strong left hand takes a fistful of wet coat, damp suit and bland tie and hauls a weathered face, lined with pain and confusion, a few feet off the floor.

"Good evening Detective Inspector," the man from the car says cheerily before landing a brutal punch with his right hand. You hear the detective inspector's nose break and recoil at the sheer malice you are witnessing.

The man in black jiggles the policeman a little, receiving a groan for his trouble. In response he lands two more vicious, full strength punches to exactly the same spot. The policeman's head lolls back, his whole form goes limp, yet the man from the car doesn't move, he seems to be thinking.

To your horror he shifts his position slightly before continuing to beat the unconscious man's face. On and on it goes, your stomach starts to shift and twist, the red, wet, slapping sounds somehow bypassing your ears and cutting straight into your gut.

NINE STOP TRIP

Eventually, finally, the man from the car seems satisfied and drops his victim to the floor like a bundle of laundry. Retrieving his weapon and straightening up, he tugs absently at his neck, surveying the extensive damage he has done. Now he steps over the detective inspector's prone form and opens a door you hadn't noticed under the stairs.

To your surprise you do not see a small, wedge shaped cupboard, but instead another flight of stairs that drop down into true, pitch darkness. The man from the car steps back to the policeman and, getting a hand under each lifeless arm, begins to haul him towards the stairs.

You turn away but can still hear the rhythmic dragging sounds. On the opposite wall you notice an array of pictures in crude, innocent crayon. While the pictures show a wide variety of people and scenes, they all share a strange, overlaid pattern of dark flecks. You realise the specks are all over the wall between the pictures as well.

The wet slapping sounds of moments earlier suddenly echo though your mind with a vengeance. In renewed horror you turn once more, just in time to see the door closing. You are alone in the grey hallway with the stains and shadows. You turn to the front door but...

...the cellar is cluttered, illuminated by a single lightbulb, bare and swinging. The disorientation is less of a problem this time, almost expected in fact. Your upstairs urge to flee is compounded by the scene now before you.

Adam Byfield

As the lightbulb's motion begins to slow the man from the car bats at it playfully. Every shadow in the room swells and shrinks sickeningly, lunging to envelop each patch of colour and texture only to fall back a heartbeat later.

The man from the car is stalking back and forth, machete in hand. You realise he is waiting for the now bare chested policeman to come round. Still spark out he seems to be leaning with surprising nonchalance, arms out, against one of the numerous wooden beams that run up from the stone floor to and across the low ceiling.

On closer inspection, and to your horror, you realise that the man from the car has nailed the other man to the beam. That strange discolouration there, that little dark shape in the centre of his forearm you've just noticed, that's the head of a nail, as are the rest of them.

For a long time the man from the car walks back and forth, occasionally moving his head against the lightbulb. You watch as he lets it roll across his brow which, you notice, bares the same bloody speckles as the hallway decor.

Eventually a groan freezes you both as the man nailed to the beam begins to wake up. You see his swollen eyes flicker, there, and again, before half opening. As his struggles to raise his head however, his breath suddenly deepens and quickens. Those eyes are now widening as the reality of his situation washes over him. Looking left and right to his arms he begins to hyperventilate and his eyes, now far too wide, look straight through you before rolling back into his head.

"No you don't," the man from the car steps forward quickly, clasping the policeman's face in his free hand. He squeezes the stained and discoloured cheeks savagely, forcing split lips into a distinctly simian pout. "We haven't got all night Detective Inspector so come on now, get with it."

Still breathing hard the defenceless man manages to focus on his assailant.

"You," he hisses simply. You're impressed at how much dignified disdain he manages to pack into this single syllable.

"That's right, me!" The man from the car is gleeful and apparently unable to contain himself, he relaxes his grip and does a twirling little dance. You watch him spin and catch your breath as he stops abruptly, the heavy blade he wields less than an inch from his captive's face. The detective inspector does not flinch.

"Me, me, me," the man from the car says, calmer now, almost philosophical. He clasps his hands, and the blade, behind his back and begins to wander in a tight circle. "So this is where I reveal to you the truth about my work. Finally I take pity on you and give you the answers you've been longing for, and you have been longing for them haven't you Detective Inspector?"

The bleeding man grimaces, he is still breathing heavily but, after a second or so, manages to say, "nope."

The man from the car smiles and adopting the stance of a fencer, places the sharp edge of his blade under his captive's chin and raises his head. "Come on now, be honest?" He tilts his own head, in line with his mocking tone.

You wait, tense, until, after a great deal of effort, the response finally comes. "Don't care why, just going to stop you." Suddenly the machete is swooping, almost catching the ceiling and now there is a deep gash across the policeman's midriff. He groans.

"No!" The man from the car's voice, suddenly harsh and bitter, fills the small, underground room. "Let's not be silly here Detective Inspector. We all know that in order to *try* and stop me you've spent the last few months *trying* to understand me."

You watch thin red strings as they trace their way downward from the dark, ugly wound. You're vaguely aware of the wound's creator swirling away only to come to a halt in a crouching position. Returning your full attention to him, you find he is grinding the tip of the machete blade into the stone floor and making a horrible sound in the process.

After a while he stops this and rests chin on hand on hand on handle before gazing up at his latest victim. "Are you real Detective Inspector? I mean, do you actually exist?" He laughs, "it's ok, you don't have to answer that. You see it doesn't occur to people like you to ask such questions does it? You're too busy working and saving and playing with your kids and screwing your wife to stop and think about it.

"I've thought about it though, oh yes, I've given that question a great deal of thought. What concerned me, you see, was that I didn't *feel* real. I couldn't find anything within myself that proved I was really here." Here he slaps the floor twice, as if to underline his words. Now he shifts to sit cross legged, resting the blade across his knees.

"Then one day, in a cafe, do you know about the cafe Detective Inspector? Probably not, I didn't kill anyone that day. Anyway, I had an epiphany. Reality, I realised, comes not from within but from others. If other people know you exist then, by that very knowing, you do. Do you see?" He doesn't wait for a response, in fact you get the impression that he's already waited a very long time to say these things.

"It didn't last however, no matter what I did, no matter how many people I convinced, the doubts always returned. The problem was of course that, once I'd pulled off my TV masterpiece..." he pauses, a proud little smile tugging at his blood splattered and yet still boring face.

"...I had nowhere left to go. What more could I do? And this was when it happened, this was when I finally stumbled upon the truth, the real, ultimate truth." He scrambles to his feet and lunges towards his audience. His lips, quivering with excitement you notice, almost touching his captive's, bruised and abused as they are.

"You see, Detective Inspector," his whispers hoarsely, "we are not real. We do not exist." Leaning back he extends his arms to mimic the policeman's pose, raising his face and voice to the ceiling. "We are in fact, nothing more than fictional characters in a book."

His head lolling the policeman manages to speak once more. "You're insane," he rasps, spitting a bloody glob onto the floor. The man from the car smiles affectionately, apparently neither surprised nor offended, before continuing.

"Do you know Detective Inspector, you are the only person besides myself to be given a speaking role in this tale? You should feel honoured, and perhaps make a little more of the privilege. Anyway, where's you deductive reasoning? Come on now, think about it.

"How on earth could I have pulled off that stunt at the museum? What about the alarms, the CCTV? And those giant red curtains tumbling from the ceiling into neatly folded piles? Wasn't it all a little impractical, a little too dramatic?" You watch uncomfortably as the policeman's thoughts run parallel to your own.

"And my grand finale, the televised personal incendiary attack, wasn't that just a little far fetched? And, for goodness sake, look at us!" He points his machete back and forth as if there could be any doubt as to whom he is referring. "The flamboyant serial killer and the hard nosed cop, could we be any more clichéd?

"No, no, my dear Detective Inspector, we are but words on a page and this," you find your teeth gritted as the machete bites into wood and a couple of fingers fall to the floor. "This only becomes real when it is read, when someone's imagination *makes* it real."

Cackling he removes another finger, the

policeman is weeping openly now, keening his pain through choking breaths. Yet another digit falls and once more the man from the car leans in close. "This can all stop you know, your pain, the horror, it can all stop in an instant, they just have to stop reading, stop imagining."

Stepping back he cocks his head on one side, as if listening for something.

"Nope, they're still here." You seem him slip the tip of the blade into the crusting slit across the policeman's belly. His tip of his tongue meanwhile, slips out in concentration as he twists the blade left and right, slowly driving it deeper. He has to raise his voice now to be heard over the coarse screams.

"They could have stopped me at any point, but they just watched it get worse and worse just like I knew they would. You see I realised that often, a story starts at its end and is then made up of flashbacks that ultimately bring the audience back to the final scene. In order to become real, to be read into some kind of existence, I just needed a grand finale." He withdraws the machete and examines the blood running from the blade.

"And what grander a finale, what more audacious a closing act, than for the serial killer to kill the very police officer chasing him in his own home? After that it was a simple matter of faith, I had only to wait in my car for it all to begin. And then suddenly, tonight, after who knows how long, it did."

You're unsure now as to whether the detective inspector is even conscious now, but the man from the car no longer seems to notice or care. He has closed his eyes and seems to be preparing himself for something.

Just before you are ready for it he lunges, swinging the machete in a great horizontal arc, spraying a slick trail of blood along the walls. The blade passes, incredibly, straight through the policeman's neck yet misses the beam behind. The man from the car releases his grip and the blades clatters off into a dark corner.

A gurgling scarlet fountain erupts from the detective inspector's twitching form, coating the lightbulb and so drowning the room in red. The man from the car throws back his head and howls with animal pleasure as the sticky darkness falls upon him.

You're aware of motion beneath you and manage to tear your gaze away from the horror to look down. The policeman's battered head has rolled to stop, his empty eyes now stare up and up and through you. Your own head feels light and clouded, part of you is still trying to make sense of what you are seeing, but the rest of you has long since given up.

For a time there is just red and noise and realisation and horror and disgust.

After that comes a strange calm, quiet as the blood drops to a more subtle flow and the man from the car catches his breath. Finally he wipes the blood from his eyes and turns. For the first time he is looking directly at you, into your eyes and through your soul. Unable to hold his gaze you lower your own and find yourself looking at that special little talisman from the car, now hanging around his neck and dripping.

"Thank you so much for this," his voice sounds surreal through it's genuine gratitude. "I knew you'd come, I knew we could do it."

He pauses, nodding and smiling.

"It's been a wild and crazy ride, come back sometime and we can do it all again."

Now he fixes you with a more serious stare.

"I'll always be here."

You stop reading.

Adam Byfield

THE i IN TEAM

He was trying not to run.

Unwilling to wrestle any further with the unruly sheaves of paper in his arms, Michael didn't check his watch but was still sure he was about to be late. He slowed slightly as a couple of other office workers rounded the corner ahead of him, only to accelerate back to a quick, twitchy stride once they passed.

Making his way through the tastefully carpeted corridors of a great and gleaming office building towards a meeting, Michael was behind schedule, as usual; despite his best efforts, as usual. What was unusual about this meeting however, was that it was the first six monthly progress review of his team's work.

Politely elbowing past a sudden knot of people, he tried not to think about it and instead cursed himself bitterly for not leaving earlier. He had never, in all six months, actually achieved his goal of arriving at a meeting ten minutes early.

That was where things happened, Michael thought, scampering stiffly down another empty length of corridor. Those idle words in lowered tones, he thought, before things start being written down, that was how it all worked. As he turned the final corner the door to the boardroom came smugly into view.

He closed his eyes, just for a second, before gritting his teeth and striding purposefully forward. By the time he reached for the handle he could feel himself starting to sweat, despite the cool, conditioned air. Wiping his palm briefly down his thigh, he gripped the chill metal and stepped into the room.

Glancing up at the clock on the wall he noticed was not actually late, but neither was he ten minutes early. There were three people sat at the large and well polished table, he noticed with relief. There should have been five including himself so at least he wasn't the last one there.

Pleasantries were exchanged as he approached an empty chair and settled his paper stack onto the mirror-like surface of the table as neatly as he could manage. His boss Caroline was there of course, talking like a machine gun into her mobile phone while her hands moved even more quickly over the laptop in front of her.

Beside her sat Dave her PA, tapping his pen against his notepad as he made small talk with the younger woman sat round the table further still. This last was Jane, another member of the team and from behind his heap of reports he eyed her and the PA with carefully concealed suspicion.

He was just wondering how much earlier than him she had arrived when Eric, their third and final team member walked in. He was a tall man who carried a dark expression beneath perpetually ruffled hair. Watching his team mate make a quick apology and take a seat, Michael marvelled once more at the familiar display of confidence.

Somehow, whenever his colleague was late for a meeting, and he often was recently, he managed to carry with him an invincible air of great importance. It was an atmosphere that suggested he could only be late for a very important reason and that in fact, people were lucky he was even there at all.

Knowing he would be the first asked to speak Michael turned his attention to the great white mass before him. By the time he had arranged several smaller and neater piles, his boss had put down her phone and closed her laptop. As she started to speak all other sounds ceased save for the frantic scratching of her PA's pen.

"Nine months ago we became aware of a new organisation, namely Hux Island, having a significant impact on several arms of our organisation. The rather eccentric business style of this new organisation, commonly known as HI, quickly became a major concern for us as we, along with all the other major players, saw our shares of the market begin to shrink." After a brief pause for breath the torrent of words continued.

"Six months ago we recruited the three of you. We did not, after all, become one of the largest and most successful commercial companies in the world by sitting on our hands. You are the Oxbridge cream of your generation, the best and the brightest. For the last two financial quarters you have had some of the best research facilities in the world at your disposal with which to develop some kind of response to this new form of competition" Caroline paused, looking sternly at the three faces in turn.

"Anyway," she said abruptly, "I should say

before we start that I'm waiting for an important call and I will have to take it should it come during this meeting." She glanced down at the sleek little mobile that sat snugly next to her dozing laptop. "Ok, let's hear it."

Knowing he was first to speak, Michael swallowed hard, fending off the urge to panic as he tried to decide whether to sit or stand. In the end he decided to remain seated and began to recite the first words of his well practiced speech for the final time.

"From their small scale beginnings to their current astronomical success, HI has made much of its main distinguishing characteristic, the so-called 'ethical factor'. Last year saw their acquisition of a mid range but high profile pharmaceutical manufacturer and this provides an excellent example of this practice." Settling into familiar ground he scooped up a couple of relevant documents from the array before him.

"It is a well documented fact that the single founder, owner and chief executive of the company receives a salary that, by contemporary corporate standards, is laughably small. In fact the salaries of the senior management team are not significantly higher than those of the workforce on the ground."

"With no shareholders and lower human resource overheads, the company appears at first glance to have quickly accumulated vast sums of capital. The 'ethical factor' becomes apparent however when considering the way in which this capital has been utilised."

Coming to the end of his introduction he smoothly distributed copies of a particularly colourful report, several pages of bright and cheery pie charts and line graphs. "In the months that followed the takeover of the pharmaceutical manufacturer, various new cosmetic ranges were launched that all proved to be very successful."

"Despite vast financial gains from this success however HI has, as you can see, made absolutely no net profit. Instead, every penny made from these popular products, after wages, manufacturing costs and forward planning, has been used to create a fund. This fund produces and distributes AIDS drugs and other medications to third world nations, particularly on the African continent, completely free of charge.

"HI funds and staffs clinics and treatment centres and has not even patented the drugs it has created, preferring instead to make the full details of how the drug can be made publicly available." Here Michael waved a densely worded document at the group.

"This practice is seen to be repeated throughout the many different business ventures HI has undertaken and has very quickly stimulated significant brand loyalty among consumers." At this point his boss interjected, however he had expected this and almost smiled as she said exactly what he had thought she would.

"This isn't sounding very positive. We're all aware of the nature of the problem, I'm still waiting to hear details of a solution." Before she could fold her arms and sit back into her chair his hands were into the piles of data.

"The thing is," he paused for effect for as long as he dare before continuing, "this new idea is not actually as novel as it appears. In fact I've found details of scores of charitable projects and co-operative organisations." Absently he patted one particular paper pile.

"Running through them all I have found a common thread. Dependent as they are on the high moral image they present, such ventures usually seem to run their course. In time another trend comes along and the consumer support wanes as the 'ethical factor' is found in new and more exciting places. Those ventures that do not actually fail usually shrink to a stable but insignificant size."

"Based on historical evidence there is no reason to believe that this new company will sustain either its growth or its current status in the long term. Simply put, the market will respond to even itself out." He tried not to let the relief show as he concluded his part of the meeting and sat back.

As Jane rose from her seat to make her presentation, he knew he should have stood up, the panic that had slowly built over the last few days began to ebb away. Far from feeling better, Michael now found himself left with the greater problem: he had no idea how they were going to beat HI.

Vaguely aware of the economic issues being outlined, he cast his mind back yet again over the last six months of research. There must be a way, he knew that, some flaw or weakness he hadn't spotted. Some obscure yet unforgivably overlooked business venture of the past must hold the key.

So far Jane hadn't mentioned anything he hadn't found for himself but he was still sure the other two had worked it out. They were probably each keeping it to themselves, both waiting for the perfect time to deliver the solution so as to take all the credit.

Movement caught his eye and he was drawn fully back to the meeting as Caroline retrieved her silent but flashing mobile from the table top. He watched as Dave scribbled down the numbers she snapped out. Eric and Jane had been discussing the subject of her suspended presentation but had now paused and were both looking directly at him.

"Isn't it?" Jane apparently repeated, a slightly exasperated look on her face. Glancing past her to Eric he found a curious but otherwise blank expression. Frowning for a second he pulled himself together and took a gamble.

"Absolutely," he decided, nodding. She seemed satisfied and turned back to continue her conversation with Eric. Michael frowned for a short while but soon enough Caroline ended her call and resumed the meeting so he was left unsure as to whether he had got away with his bluff.

As the presentation continued, ended and was replaced by another, he lapsed back into his funk. Why couldn't he see it? He wasn't saying anything new either, not really, but the more

NINE STOP TRIP

Michael listened, the more certain he became that Eric was holding something back.

The meeting finally came to and end with the three of them receiving a scathing review and being told, in a biting tone, that the next presentations would now be in *three* months and that they'd better have something more to say for themselves next time.

As the others drifted from the room Michael began to arrange his papers, collecting those carelessly left behind by the others. Having stacked them into two drunken looking piles, he was about to stoop forward and gather them up but paused instead.

For a moment Michael stood and imagined how it would feel to throw all that paper up in the air and simply walk away through the floating white. A small smile flickered across his face before he took a deep breath and hauled the stacks up into his arms. Adjusting himself to the bulk and the weight he turned and made his way steadily from the now empty room.

After three or four minutes he managed to close the door behind him.

She was trying not to yawn.

Getting to the meeting early had seemed like a good idea earlier in the day. It demonstrated enthusiasm, dedication and good time management skills, or so she had thought. In practice however, Jane now found herself trapped in mindless small talk with Dave, her boss's PA and one of the dullest of all the sleazy little men at the office.

Watching the clock as it made its painfully slow progress she was finally, eventually and thankfully pleased to see the door open. In came Michael, the shorter of her two male colleagues, obscured as usual by a mountain of papers and reports. He was right on time, to the second, just like always. You really could set your watch by him Jane thought enviously.

As Michael settled his work onto the table and himself down beside it, she glanced down at her own meagre notes. The guy was a research machine. If any of the three of them could have succeeded in their task it would surely have been him; but of course Jane knew that none of them had.

At this point the door opened again and her other colleague Eric entered the room. He was late, Jane noted, and his hair was a mess, but somehow he made it seem like these things were unavoidable and took his seat with the air of a man with many other more important things to do.

After some predictable preamble from the Caroline, Michael began his presentation from behind his array of neat little paper islands. Jane half listened, just in case he had found something extraordinary, she still couldn't quite put it past him, but was relieved to hear only familiar facts, figures and arguments.

He hadn't found anything, she knew, accepting a colourful handout, he couldn't have.

NINE STOP TRIP

Jane hadn't been with the company very long when she realised what their real task was. There was no solution to the problem facing their corporate employers, she had satisfied herself of this after the first month and a half.

Jane knew that the company was, ultimately, doomed. Although the practices of their new rival didn't make a lot of sense to her, she recognised that her employers simply could not compete with the unprecedented consumer enthusiasm HI had somehow developed.

Jane also knew however, that there was still time enough for her to climb the ranks and accumulate some insurance for when that fall finally came. All she had to do in the meantime was tell her employers what they wanted to hear and leave out the rest.

With this in mind Jane stood to begin her own presentation. "My own area of research has been a detailed study of HI's economic efficiency. By building up a detailed model of how their business works; of what it does and more importantly does not do, on a day to day basis; I have managed to identify key areas of failure in HI's organisation."

"A study of the company's accounts for the last financial year shows an abject lack of even the most basic tax efficiencies. No real effort appears to have been made to minimise tax costs and the few beneficial steps that were evident could all be explained by other, more likely motivations."

Caroline was frowning but seemed

interested none the less.

"HI's real weakness however, runs far deeper than some apathetic accounting and relates to the kind of 'ethical' schemes we've already heard some mention of. The example that best demonstrates this weakness, is HI's recent takeover of one of the smaller national power companies."

"Their very first act was to begin implementation of a large scale, and patently financially unsound, scheme to change their generating plants to bio fuels. Such bold yet reckless steps are perhaps what we are becoming to expect of our new rival, however in this instance they have gone further still."

"Several factories from one of HI's manufacturing arms have taken orders from the power company for..."

Jane noticed the phone's enthusiastic flashing before Caroline did. Glancing toward Eric, who rolled his eyes, she turned and sat against the edge of the table.

"You're talking about the Community..." Eric muttered.

"...Electricity Grant, yes. Well I was," she returned the roll of the eyes.

"I take it you're not impressed?" Eric's expression gave away nothing.

"No, I'm not impressed, it's like..." Jane stopped herself, wanting to keep her planned words fresh. "It's the most ridiculous business idea ever," she decided on, turning to their so far silent colleague. "Isn't it?"

"Absolutely," Michael replied knowingly and nodded.

"See?" She turned back to face Eric, "and Michael would know, he's spent the last six months researching them."

"Ok, but what exactly is so crazy about it?" Eric asked quietly, quite obviously trying to tease her now. Despite herself, Jane snapped back at him.

"An electricity supplier giving free energy saving light bulbs to its customers?..."

"Thanks for that Claire," Caroline said, cutting Jane off and ending her call. She had a brief and muttered conversation with Dave before turning back to the table. "Sorry about that, please continue."

"As I was saying, several factories from one of HI's manufacturing arms have taken orders from the power company for energy saving light bulbs and various other energy efficiency goods. These are then being distributed en mass to all customers free of charge as part of the company's so called *Community Electricity Grant*"

"Simply put, through the CE Grant, HI has acquired complete control over supply with one hand while acting to reduce demand with the other. Overall they have increased their outgoings while reducing their revenue and there is quite simply no way that HI can make money."

"This practice can be found across the board in their various other business ventures and leads me to agree with Michael. While they may currently be riding a wave of good publicity, HI's economic systems just cannot hold up long term."

Taking her seat Jane felt satisfied with the smokescreen she had put up and wondered idly if the other two were panicking. It must be strange for them, she thought, being used to coming top of their classes, being the best, and yet finding themselves completely unable to solve the problem they were being paid to consider.

As Eric stood to present his own take on the situation, Jane reflected on the differences between herself and the two young men she worked with. Firstly, she thought, they both trusted authority. If they were told there was an answer, they would believe it and keep looking.

At the same time however, they were both so self confident. What must they be thinking now then, unable to doubt either their instructions or themselves? Surely the only answer for them, certainly the only one she could think of for them anyway, was that the problem must actually be far more complex than it appeared.

Having seemed to leap forward during her own presentation, the clock had now returned to its original, painfully lethargic pace. Jane half listened to the final presentation, just to be sure of no surprises, but nothing was said to prove her assumptions wrong.

Caroline spent a moment or two looking over the notes she had made during their presentations before eyeing each one of them venomously in turn. '"Well," she began in a biting tone, "I have to say I'm not impressed. You're supposed to be the best your generation has to offer and yet even given six months with some of the best research facilities in the world, not one of you has delivered on the original task set to you."

"I've never made a secret of the fact that, from the very beginning I felt this, *thinktank*, " this last word appeared to carry a sour taste as she spat it across the table, "was a waste of money. We were well aware of the nature of the situation six months when we hired you. In fact our awareness of the situation was the very *reason* we hired you!

"Clearly you all need to be reminded of the task in hand, namely that of ultimately presenting the board with a selection of valid plans of action from which to chose. Plans of action with which to respond to this new, Hux Island challenge. In light of your failure to do so I'm going to suggest we meet again in three months time rather than six, David if you could arrange that please." Dave scribbled away furiously beside her.

"If at this next meeting I am not satisfied that you have all made significant progress towards the goal you have been set, your contracts will have to be reviewed. Now I suggest you all return to your respective departments and make a start."

With this Caroline gathered her things and left, Dave in tow. The ultimatum was fine with her, Jane thought, as she gathered her things and made to leave. It gave her plenty of time to come up with some more pacifying hot air. Glancing over her shoulder as she approached the door she noted Michael quietly gathering up his papers.

Jane noticed she was still holding the handout he had distributed during his presentation. Resolving to return it to him later in the day, she hurried through the door and away from her boss's PA who was again trying to catch her eye.

Looking up and down the corridor, as if about to cross a busy road, she found that Eric was nowhere to be seen. She had wanted to return some of the jabs he had landed during the break in her presentation but it would keep, Jane thought, and anyway, she knew where she could find him.

He was trying not to get angry.

Sat at his desk, Eric watched the clock march on, one twitch after another, each telling him he would now be even later for the meeting. He had spent the last six months trying to predict the future of Hux Island, his employers latest rival, in order to help destroy them. The problem was that, after five and a half months of scratching his head, he finally did understand the nature of Hux Island, only it wasn't quite what he had expected.

Eric now found himself questioning not only his current occupation but his last decade and a half of formal education. Looking about him, every piece of office furniture and equipment now seemed to glow with an unholy light, garishly reminding him of his own naivety and outright foolishness.

NINE STOP TRIP

Despite it all however, and this was what was driving him crazy, Eric found still couldn't quite turn his back on what was, until recently, the only world he had ever known. How could he go and present his boss with a business strategy when he didn't actually want the company to succeed? At the same time however, how could he walk away from everything he had been taught? Everything he'd worked so hard to achieve?

Snatching up his notes in frustration, Eric stalked through the corridors towards the boardroom, cursing himself with every step. Opening the door he found the face of the clock, and four others, waiting for him. The first told him he was late and the others all seemed to agree.

Taking his seat it occurred to Eric that he should probably be feeling something in this situation, panic or guilt perhaps. As Caroline began the meeting however, he found he just couldn't bring himself to care. He ran a hand through his hair, so carefully gelled into the latest pseudo-scruffy style and sighed as Michael began his presentation.

Eyeing the heaps of paper across the table, Eric really had to hand it to him, he was good. When it came to research Michael seemed to have some kind of natural ability. He was further distracted by the specific information on offer however and he found himself thinking about how it had used to feel to believe such things.

Hearing the familiar facts, figures and arguments now felt like suddenly noticing another instrument playing for the first time in his all time favourite song. Watching Michael deliver the material however, he had to admit the guy seemed genuinely enthused.

As time plodded on Eric became less and less interested in what his colleagues were saying and more with how they felt about it. When Jane's presentation was interrupted by Caroline's mobile phone he met her eyes, rolling his own in sympathy.

She'd just been broaching the very subject that had led Eric to his dramatic change of mindset and he was eager to try and regain a brief glimpse of his previous perspective. Waiting for Jane to settle on the edge of the table he leaned in and asked in lowered tones, "You're talking about the Community..."

"...Electricity Grant, yes. Well I was," she returned his roll of the eyes.

"I take it you're not impressed?" If he could only see things as she did, as he used to, just for a moment, he'd be able to compare, make a logical decision. If not he was left with nothing but a leap of faith.

"No, I'm not impressed, it's like..." Jane paused and he suspected she was struggling to express the idea without wrapping it in business jargon.

"It's the most ridiculous business idea ever," she finally continued, turning away from him towards Michael. "Isn't it?" She asked him.

"Absolutely," Michael replied knowingly and nodded.

"See?" Jane turned back to face him, "and Michael would know, he's spent the last six months researching them."

Yes, they both really believed it Eric decided. But how could he explain to them the way in which he had recently come to see things? Perhaps if they followed the same path he had taken, worked through the same arguments they would come to the same place. Eric had begun by examining what appeared to be the long term flaws of HI's business tactics.

"Ok," he tried, "but what exactly is so crazy about it?" To his surprise Jane snapped back at him almost immediately.

"An electricity supplier giving free energy saving lightbulbs to its customers?..." But here Caroline ended her call and resumed the meeting, snatching away his opportunity. As Jane resumed her presentation he began to focus more on the matters in hand.

Regardless of his sudden crisis of conscience in just a few minutes he would have to give an enthusiastic presentation extolling the dominance of his employers over their new rival. Eric read through his notes as casually as he could, vaguely aware of Jane's economic analysis washing over him. He'd just about prepared himself for what he had to say when he noticed the expectant silence that had settled about him. Taking a breath he stood and looked briefly round the table before starting to speak.

"My work of the last six months has focussed on long term socio-economic projections. One particular area of interest has been to consider the implications of the unprecedented brand loyalty Hux Island have cultivated via the various practices described by my colleagues."

His tongue flicked over dry lips as he continued.

"In fact a worrying preliminary finding suggests that so powerful is this phenomenon it may actually prove sufficient to overcome the various weaknesses we've heard outlined today. Past models of consumer trend behaviour may not be entirely valid for such a successful venture. In turn this success suggests that our rivals will be able to expand their markets quickly enough to counter the economic flaws described."

Eric had been concerned that his colleagues may take issue with his apparent marginalizing of their arguments but both seemed to be listening happily.

"Thankfully," he began again but found he had to stop and clear this throat, "these findings are all bound by limited timescales, beyond which the aforementioned arguments come back into force. As we've already heard, our rival is seeking to reduce demand among consumers across the board while investing in less profitable, more sustainable working practices."

"Some analysts have gone so far as to suggest that HI is gradually changing the nature of the nation's infrastructure, moving it away from a commercial base. Now assuming for the moment that such a thing were possible, and there is a strong body of opinion that refutes this, the question is what would happen were it to be achieved?"

"Clearly a reduction in commercial productivity would actually result in huge job losses. This further reduce HI's available consumer base and thereby exacerbates the problem. However it would also do great damage to the reputation on which their whole venture appears to balance."

Pausing for both effect and breath, Eric realised he could taste bile.

"The very worst case scenario would see HI rise to almost total dominance before collapsing under its own weight to leave a void. At this point the market would reassert itself and the trend would turn back to," yet another word caught in his throat, "normality.

"In the short term it would seem, from the point of view of statistical projection, unwise to attempt to compete directly with our rival in terms of 'ethical kudos', but this is definitely the area that needs to be targeted, in some way, in order to regain dominance of the market.

"Another potentially significant factor considers that HI must also be aware of the long term consequences of their actions. This clearly suggests that, rather than blazing some grand and noble trail, HI may actually be aiming for nothing more than a lucrative short term investment."

After a brief smile that only affected the bottom half of his face, Eric took his seat. As Caroline delivered her verdict he found all he could think about was getting home and having a shower. He was somewhat taken aback by the toll the presentation had taken on him. Who knew speaking words he disagreed with could be so hard?

Hux Island had looked ahead alright, an obscure essay he had found written by the founder had made that obvious to him. In that same essay he had found the key to the puzzle: the company was not intended to make money. In fact it served no other purpose than to fundamentally shift society's focus.

The long term plan hinted towards in the piece seemed include some form of major shift in direction in the future. Having established "sufficient changes in social infrastructure", whatever that meant, the company would shift into logistical and information support services for the millions of small scale independent businesses it predicted would emerge.

The new economic climate would be geared entirely towards minor local businesses and, in fact, the large corporate structures that formed the contemporary norm would be cost prohibitive under this system. He remembered the very first time he'd read the piece he'd actually laughed out loud. After the last couple of weeks however it suddenly didn't seem quite so funny anymore.

Caroline had apparently finished, as had the meeting, and so he made his way to the door as quickly as possible. Striding down the corridor towards his office the thought of a shower still played on Eric's mind. Reaching a choice of corners to turn, he suddenly opted to head away from his office and towards the exit.

Eric's heart pounded as he approached the glass doors, two great glowing hints of the daylight beyond, and a slightly manic smile appeared on his face. He was actually doing it, he was actually walking out, leaving everything he had worked for behind him. Luckily he had a pretty good idea of someone else he might like to work for.

THE STORY

The drive had been long, frustrating and entirely not worth it. Unlike some country lanes, which were obviously not built with cars in mind, the road that had finally brought her to the village appeared to have been constructed specifically to make driving as difficult as possible.

It had seemed to her, as the night closed in around her fashionable little car, that each mile closer to the village had required two miles of deviously twisted road. Five minutes after leaving the main road she had not only lost count of how many blind corners and hidden dips she had negotiated but had also lost all sense of direction.

With a sigh she turned out the bedside lamp and stared up into the darkness. Coming round yet another sharp bend in the road she had suddenly found herself between the school and church and that signified she had reached the village. Far too tired for relief she had come across the guesthouse almost immediately after and just minutes later she had collapsed into an ancient but comfortable bed.

As her body began to relax it dragged her mind towards sleep and, approaching that hazy threshold, previously ignored thoughts floated across the backs of her finally closing eyes. Her first day at the paper; her and Craig both fresh faced and eager; that thrill of a dream becoming real; the excitement of opportunity and the phone call to her parents. A chill halted her drowsing progress, had that really been almost a year ago?

NINE STOP TRIP

She opened her eyes only to find another shade of darkness.

Where was Craig now? Down on the south coast at a party conference, that bastard. Rolling over she pulled at the pillows in annoyance. It was because she was a woman, and because Craig sucked up to the editor, and because he had happened to be in the right place at the right time, it was all so unfair. Her silent ranting over she finally listened to the whisper that had waited so patiently, maybe he was just better journalist.

Her frown was stretched and broken by a deep yawn. No, she was good at what she did. She knew that and if they didn't, well then she would prove it. Even this tiny village must have stories more interesting than award winning pottery. Tomorrow she'd find them, her dues would be paid and she'd never get another of these crappy little assignments again. For the first time she realised that she could hear the tide and it wasn't long before she fell into it's rhythm and was swept away into the restful realms of sleep.

The morning was bright and not unpleasantly cool. Having raced through a light breakfast she headed out into the village carrying and excited sparkle in her eyes. She had a meeting arranged with the owner of the local pottery firm but this was not the focus of her thoughts. How could it be after what she had seen just hours earlier?

A few buildings clung to a typically sharp sweep of road that lingered briefly before lurching back out into open country. The bulk of the village lay between the road and the seafront, squat cottages seemingly growing out of the steep slope in random clumps to enclose tiny, twisting lanes. As she negotiated these ever downwards towards the smell, and eventual sight, of the sea, she replayed the scene from the previous night.

Upon awaking there had been immediate questions to answer. Having established where she was she had moved on to the next. What had woken her? Becoming more aware of the world around her she had lain perfectly still, listening intently to the darkness and the sea. Just as sleep began to tug at her sleeve it came again, a voice. Distance sapped its strength and the tide crushed the words, but a voice it was.

Slipping from beneath blankets patiently warmed and shaped, she had crept the three steps to the window and gingerly moved the curtain's edge. The guesthouse sat on the road and atop the hill, giving a wide daytime view. The deep rural night reduced this to greys and shadows and, with her first glance, it seemed that she could barely find the horizon let alone the mysterious speaker.

As if pandering to her struggle a tiny light had shuddered into view. After a few moments following its path she realised that it was a torch or lantern being carried by the speaker. The night had nipped at her neck and reminded her of the warm comfort so close behind but, casting sleep aside, she had held her breath and watched.

A line of figures had made slow progress along the beach. Each figure had carried a light and somehow the sight had seemed to clarify the sound so that she recognised a rhythm to the murmuring.

Despite their apparently casual pace the line had passed quickly from view, however this had been time enough for a chill to seep deep into her limbs. Back in bed she had smiled up into the darkness, this was it! Be it illegal immigrant workers, drug smugglers or illegal immigrant workers smuggling drugs, this was the story she had been about to go looking for, she was sure of it.

She would have to be careful and at her best. If the gangmasters, or smugglers or whatever, thought she was onto them, they could relocate to any one of the dozens of other little villages that dotted the coast and she would miss her chance. Sleep had struggled to overcome excitement, but finally succeeded and she had slept the rest of the night beneath blankets and warm fantasies of success.

Emerging from between two rows of dark yet cosy cottages she found herself confronted by a small harbour and a long pile of rocks posing as a beach. Of the two modest benches available she chose the one that gave the best view of the 'beach'. The tide was in and she noted with interest that beyond the seafront a headland reached out into the heaving grey. A large cave undermined the outcrop, the mouth of which was receiving blow after blow from the great waves that knocked out white teeth of spray with each strike.

Glancing back up over the cascading roofs she could make out the guest house and realised that the figures she had seen had been moving from the cave end of the beach towards the harbour. The tide had been out and so it seemed reasonable, if not obvious, that they had conducted whatever their business was within the cave before heading back up into the village.

The 'tourist information guide' she had picked up in the guest house was in fact a single sheet of folded A4, bearing simple black type and no photographs. The back page sported a tide chart and the next low tide replaced the potter's interview as her most significant forthcoming appointment. She sat by the harbour a while longer, reading the brief history of the village before simply breathing the air and watching the water.

As with anywhere in the village, the potter's house was just a short walk from the harbour. Nethergate Road was near the top of the hill, relatively flat and looked just like the rest of the village. It wasn't until she actually saw the well weathered street sign that the name struck her as unusual. Such names were usually found in large towns that had been in some way fortified in the past. In the city she called her home the road that had once led to the church gate had become Kirkgate and that to the bridge gate, Briggate. Surely this village had never warranted any kind of gate and even if it had, what the hell was a 'nether' gate?

She was pondering this when she heard a feline call at her feet. Looking down she was confronted by the biggest housecat she had ever seen. The ginger tom that stood before her demanding attention was not especially fat or fluffy, he was just enormous. As he rubbed himself against her legs she saw that his back came up to her knee and when she squatted down to stroke him he almost knocked her over. "Hello there," she cooed to him, "what on earth do they feed you eh?" Looking out over the water and tiny boats below she muttered, more to herself than to the cat, "nothing on earth I suppose."

Together they continued along the road until she found herself in front of yet another stout cottage. Setting it apart from the rest however, a sign hung above this door baring the simple design of a crab holding what appeared to be a backwards **S** above its head.

The starting-to-be-renowned logo of the village's award winning pottery reminded her of the job she was there to do and so, taking a thick pad from her shoulder bag, she approached the open door and knocked. Minutes later and she was sat in the surprisingly spacious first floor workroom surrounded by the tools and ceramics of the literal cottage industry. Smiling her thanks she accepted an especially elegant mug of tea and settled into the familiar routine.

She asked the questions she had prepared and received the answers she had expected. The potter was a tall man whose weathered face was partially covered by a neatly trimmed beard. His bright eyes watched her with a casual intensity as he answered her questions in a soft voice that echoed an easy confidence. Not wanting to ask she tried to gauge the man's age but found herself at a loss, though despite this, he seemed younger than she had expected.

Reaching her final scripted question she caught herself glancing at his left hand. His fingers carried dried clay but no ring, though he'd probably take it off to work wouldn't he. Focussing she drained her tea and got on with the job in hand.

"Of course the durability of your pottery has attracted almost as much attention as the design. No-one's been able to work out how you make it so strong. So what's the secret?" she smiled.

Returning the smile from within his beard the potter shifted in his chair and laughed quietly. "Experience," he said after a moments thought. The silence that followed was not uncomfortable but suggested that he would not be drawn on the subject. and as she hadn't expected him to actually reveal the secret she let the question go. Looking down into the curls of her handwriting and the empty space she had reached, she took a breath and smiled again. Time to dig a little deeper.

"So what about the future?" she asked,

pretending to consider her notes.

"The future?" he returned the question almost immediately.

"Well, many rural communities are dying out. The kids grow up and move to the cities, the parents retire..." she let the pause ask the question.

"Oh I see," he chuckled, "we don't have that problem."

"You don't?" she replied, surprised for the first time.

"No, we're all very happy here. Our children are perfectly content to stay and have children of their own."

"Surely some of them are tempted by the opportunities and excitement of the cities," his absolute answer had intrigued her.

"I'm sure some of them are tempted but as I said, we're content here and that's worth more than bright lights and money."

"Contentment huh?" she frowned a smile, "so maybe that's the secret of your pottery?"

His laughter seemed out of proportion to her comment but didn't last long. "Yes I suppose it is." Somehow she'd lost track and so tried to turn the conversation back.

"So there're none of the typical problems of manpower and income then." The potter held her gaze until she retreated once more to consider her invisible notes.

"You know, I've lived by the sea all my life..." he said finally, his own pause drawing her eyes back to his, "and I know fishing when I see it." Suddenly the room did seem small after all, and the refreshing sea breeze carried a previously unnoticed chill.

"I, ah..." she stalled with a nervous laugh. "Anyway, what with this award and everything I'm sure our readers will be interested to see your handiwork for themselves. What's the easiest way to purchase a piece?" Cursing herself she feigned interest in her own knee-jerk question.

"Just go to the website, they can see the catalogue and there's secure online ordering."

"There's a website?" Hearing the surprise in her own voice she doubled her curses.

"Yes, we have a website. We're locals, not yokels." Tickled by his perfect soundbite she mirrored his gentle smile with one of relief. Apparently he hadn't taken offence.

"Look," he said rising from his chair, signifying the end of the interview, "it's the final of the Sea Queen contest later on. You're obviously as interested in the workings of our village as in those of my kiln, so why don't you come along?"

After two such hideous faux pas she couldn't have said no if she'd tried and it wasn't until after she had left the potter's home that she realised that attending the local beauty pageant meant she would miss low tide. Shaking her head and swearing vehemently below her breath she headed back to the guesthouse. As she turned off Nethergate Road the ginger tom, and his equally huge tortoise shell friend, watched her go.

NINE STOP TRIP

The town hall stood alone at the end of the road, just along from the potter's cottage and she arrived just in time for the initial formalities of the contest. Though the potter and the elderly lady from the guesthouse were the only villagers she had actually met, everyone seemed to know who she was and she was welcomed with smiles as a space shuffled open for her on the back bench of the packed hall.

The 'hall' was actually more of a large room and featured a simple low stage at one end. Feigning interest in the procession of young women in their best dresses soon proved too much and her gaze left the stage. Looking around she saw only one other exit beside the small front door through which she had entered, a second door off to her right. Her eyes drifted over the backs of heads before and the faces to the side. The potter caught her eye and nodded a greeting which she answered with a smile.

Since waking, thoughts of the big story hidden within this little village had not left her for a moment. Now however, witnessing such concentration and civic pride all around her, she began to grudgingly admit that perhaps this was, after all, just a simple and happy village, with award winning pottery. Her big break would have to come from somewhere else, perhaps the next dull little story she was bound to cover.

The contestants took their turns to captivate the audience with their party pieces and to pass the time she studied the villagers more closely. It wasn't until the third potential Sea Queen began twirling a baton that she realised what it was about these people that was beginning to strike her as odd.

Every single person in the room was a picture of health. All tall with long, strong limbs, their skin and hair seemed to glow. There was no glamour or unusual beauty about these quite obviously ordinary people, just an of aura of great strength and vitality. The ginger tom sprang to her mind and she remembered how sleek and shiny his coat had been.

As the hard bench beneath her became increasingly uncomfortable the contest drew to a close and though she hadn't really been paying attention, she presumed that the girl taking pride of place in the centre of the stage was this year's Sea Queen. The crowd stood excitedly and applause swelled to fill the modest building. Welcoming the chance to stretch her legs and rest her behind she rose with them, just in time to notice the potter lead a group of villagers through that other door.

In an instant her career changing scoop was back on.

She asked the woman to her left where the toilet was and, to her delight, was directed to the very same door. Smiling and nodding she made her way through the beaming crowd and slipped through into a quiet and dimly lit corridor. The toilet did indeed lie just ahead but the corridor continued to the head of a staircase.

NINE STOP TRIP

Creeping all the way, she listened desperately for any sound other than the murmur of the crowd but her own heart was all she could find. Silence and darkness met her at the top of the stairs and she hesitated for only a moment before descending.

Running her hand along the wall to her left she felt her way down the stairs as they twisted around on themselves. Initially she had presumed that she would find herself in the cellar of the hall but the stairs just seemed to keep going. Both staircase and walls now seemed to be carved out of the solid bedrock and, for a moment, she considered how far underground she must be before an echo of claustrophobia caused her to banish such thoughts.

Finally she stumbled onto the flat. After a moments careful probing she found herself in a corridor just three feet wide though tall enough for her to stand comfortably. Again she strained her ears and again she heard nothing but her own heart. She did notice, however, that the air was fresh and mobile. Her palms flat against the deeply cold rock she pressed on blindly into the black and gentle breeze.

Her vision redundant her mind's eye tried to place herself under the village but she couldn't even tell which direction the spiral stairs had finally sent her in. After what seemed like ages in the dark she finally saw a flickering hint of illumination ahead. Her shallow breaths and steps both ceased as her ears reached out to the light. A chilled spark leapt from the walls to her spine as a familiar murmuring was carried to her along a faint tidal rhythm.

Of course! This passage must lead down through the cliffs to the cave she had seen earlier. A perfect smugglers hideaway! Licking her suddenly dry lips she resumed her creeping pace and found that the corridor terminated in a sharp left turn. Crouching, she pressed herself against the stone and peered round the corner, revealing as little of herself as she could.

A large domed cave lay before her, the roof disappearing up into blackness. A few feet away she could make out the silhouette of a few squat rocks emerging from an otherwise smooth floor and off to the stood the villagers. Frowning she struggled to accept what her eyes strained to tell her. The villagers were stood in neat rows facing her, each holding a thick, ugly candle. Though she could clearly see their faces they were too distracted to pick hers out of the shadows.

Standing with his back to her, the potter stood before the crowd wearing an ankle length black robe. This wasn't smuggling, drugs, people or otherwise. This was... what was this? As her legs began to deaden the cave sprang to life once more as the potter continued his recitation.

"Oh great father we call to you,"
"We call to you," echoed the solemn crowd.
"Oh timeless father we give praise to you,"
"We praise you,"
"And for your gifts to us we thank you,"
"We thank you,"

NINE STOP TRIP

"For you, oh mighty father, though you dwell beneath the seas, you have given us all that we are,"
"All that we are,"
"And all that we need,"
"All that we need,"
"And so we call to you,"
"We call to you."

Noticing, and retrieving, her awe struck fallen jaw, she watched as the villagers sank to their knees and promptly bowed their heads. For a few moments the distant sound of the tide filled the cave before the potter spoke once more.

"And so we call the names. Almighty Poseidon..." he began,
"...come to us," the kneeling villagers concluded.
"All knowing Neptune..."
"...come to us."
"Oh timeless Dagon..."
"... come to us."

The names continued to flow though their forms became stranger and stranger until it seemed to her that the potter was ending his phrases with strange and voweless sounds. So engrossed was the congregation that she managed to convince her shaking form to make the brief and crouching dash to the deep shadows behind the rocks.

From her new vantage she could see that the candles, still clasped in praying hands, appeared to be formed from a black, green sludge-like wax and as they burned they filled the cave with a pungent, fishlike aroma that she hadn't noticed before. Heads bowed and eyes closed, the villagers continued their mantra. Even now, bathed in the sickly candle light, she couldn't find a flaw in their appearance.

Her heart pounded in her ears as the mantra lulled her focus. This was still a story, not the one she had been expecting, but a story none the less. Perhaps she could tie it in with the fall in church attendance, people returning to pagan rites as modern religion fails. Or maybe she could sell it as a backlash against a society increasingly obsessed with technology.

A final droning plea apparently ended the kneeling part of the ceremony and the villagers lithely returned to their feet. The sound of the tide and the smell of the candles dragged her back to the moment, as she waited and hoped for something a little more outrageous to expose. She was disappointed to hear the potter launch into yet another round of ceremonial verse.

"Oh great father we call your names,
That you may be amongst us,
And share with us your knowledge vast,
In scraps that we may bare.
For when all the lands of the earth were one,
You did reign upon them,
And over cities great of peoples true,
You did sit on high.
Though the lands were torn and you did fall,

NINE STOP TRIP

To sleep beneath the seas,
You remain, oh endless one,
Your magicks know not time.
You spoke unto the first of men,
That the keepers of your names,
Shall be ravaged not by the hands of time,
But will know the ancient skills.
Your ocean realm provides for us,
All that we might need,
And so great father we call your names,
That you may be amongst us."

A communal murmur concluded the prayer and the villagers visibly relaxed. To her dismay they began to file towards the corridor entrance off to her right. There had been no orgy, no violence or drugs and not a single animal sacrifice. Turning to rest her back against the damp rock she shook her head. The damned pottery had been more interesting for god's sake! Disappointment settled over her as she waited for the cave to empty so she could leave and thoughts of Craig interviewing politicians taunted her.

So vivid was her daydream that it took her several seconds to realise that the villagers were not leaving the cave. The first she knew of this was when her peripheral vision suddenly screamed the appearance of the head of a line to her left. Gasping she began to move to find another line appearing from the right. Talking casually among themselves the villagers filed round the edge of the cave to line the arc of its back wall before stopping and turning to face her!

The candles they still carried chased her shadowy protection away and she found herself crouching at the centre of a now silent nightmare horseshoe. Legs and lungs suddenly hollow, she struggled to stand or speak. Though her eyes were wider than ever before, she couldn't take in all that she saw. Between her and the villagers gaped the mouth of pit, previously hidden in the pitch darkness. It occurred to her how lucky she had been not to accidentally find it earlier until her brain screamed at her to focus on more immediate matters.

Her mouth began to move, waiting for words to deliver, but before she could find them the potter's voice boomed behind her. In one fluid motion her shoulders reached her ears and she spun round on the spot. Stood atop the rocks the potter loomed above her, his robes flowing around him as if dancing to his words.

"Oh great father of the sea we welcome you,
And give to you your queen..."

NINE STOP TRIP

B
  E
    A
  U
  T
  Y

To whoever finds this,

    I am about to take my own life in the attic bedroom of this house. By the time this note is discovered, I will be dead. Please call the emergency services and inform them that there is a body at this address. Under no circumstances venture upstairs yourself.

    The attached, typewritten letter describes what has happened to me over the past few weeks and why I have decided to end my life. Please pass this on to the police upon their arrival. I thank you and apologise for any emotional distress this situation may cause you.

E Christie

Looking back I am unsure where to begin. It's almost three weeks ago to the day that I saw **her** for the very first time, but this didn't start there. I hadn't been happy for a long time, plodding through my days like a machine. I'd go to work and count down the hours until I could leave. Then, I'd go home to bed and count down the hours until I had to be at work.

That day hadn't been anything special. I'd risen with the usual nausea and begun the routine once more. I shivered as I washed and dressed and the dull, grey daylight hurt my eyes as I left the house and set off along the usual route.

147

Round the corner and past the taxi rank to the pub, I hunched my shoulders about my ears to fend off the early morning chill.

Over the road, past the school and up that bastard hill. Every day I would try to lose myself in some daydream or other so as not to think about the day's work ahead or the constant protests of my body as I leaned into the incline. Try as I might I never could shift that feeling of dread and so, instead, I would carry it to work with me. Reaching the top of that damn hill I would walk along the edge of the park and try to enjoy the shape of the trees, but even this seemed beyond me.

Without sleep the days just blurred together into one long twilight and everything I had left that morning went into keeping one foot in front of the other. I remember I glanced at my watch as I reached the university campus and, to my horror, realised that I needed to pick up the pace if I were to avoid being late, again. There were still very few people about and certainly no students at this time in the morning. Remembering my own days at university with bitter envy I hurried on towards the main road.

By this point I had found my regular rhythm and silent marching song. Fuck-the-job. Walk-a-way. This familiar mantra was always percussive along the quiet street, but never fully persuasive. A rash of grey and well chewed spots gave the pavement a diseased look and signalled my immanent arrival in the city centre. Over the bridge and down past the supermarket and I was nearly there. By now I was walking among people and, as usual, found myself to be resigned to the day ahead. Cutting behind the bank I crossed the loop road and headed down the cobbled arcade that would deliver me into the arms of my employer.

At that moment I honestly thought that there was nothing in this world that could haul me up out of the grey shadows I had made my home. Staring at the cobbles beneath my feet as I was, I almost didn't see her at all. (My god, just think!) As it happened she was talking into a mobile phone and it was her voice alone that lifted my eyes from the ground.

Glancing up I could only have seen her for a second before she passed me. It was the longest second of my life. I seemed to see her all at once and remember the details afterwards. Quite simply, I was overwhelmed by that instant, not even turning my head as she passed. Instead I could only focus on her image, now freshly burned into my weary eye.

The colour and texture of her hair and the way it fell about her face. Her face, it's shape and tone, the cheeks, jaw and nose, all framing her eyes. Her eyes, so deep and yet so bright, rich colour matching the business suit she wore.

I approached work in a newfound daze. Unlike my previous stupor, I now felt elated and somehow alive in a way that I had not upon waking. Long forgotten feelings stirred within me and, out of nowhere, I felt a smile tug at the perpetual frown I wore. Curiosity, desire, and even hope were my companions during that early shift. I didn't check my watch once all day, distracted as I was, and before I knew it I was walking back into that arcade on my way home. I can remember it all so clearly, it really does seem like yesterday and yet so much has happened since.

That night, I slept, and I mean I really slept. Real, restful sleep. It was just amazing. For the next day or two I walked to work fully alert, following the same old route eagerly now, chasing hope all the way. But I didn't see her. I stopped sleeping again and fell into an even deeper funk than before. I felt somehow cheated.

Then, one night a couple of weeks ago, I was on my way home from a particularly dull day and there she was. I couldn't believe it, she was standing at a bus stop talking to a couple of guys. As I approached I worked hard to appear thoroughly casual and was relieved to see that the conversation seemed purely platonic. The two men were labourers of some kind and wore heavy sand coloured boots. That she was dressed similarly didn't seem strange at the time. It looked amazing on her, just as the suit had and I think I actually held my breath as she said her goodbyes and walked straight past me.

Not missing a step I just kept going as if nothing had happened but, as I passed the bus stop, I caught part of the conversation she had left to the two men. "What's he like eh?" said the larger of the two, while the shorter one had said nothing and simply shaken his head. At the time all I could think of was her. I feasted greedily on that warm feeling I got from seeing her. That was all I wanted to know about just then.

NINE STOP TRIP

Full of expectation I went to bed a full hour earlier than usual that night. Laying there, enjoying the feeling, I tried to ignore my fear of losing it again and settle down to sleep. This was when I finally thought about what the man had said. Of course they could have been talking about anyone, or I could have just misheard him, but I couldn't shake the feeling that they were talking about her. I won't tell you the things that went through my mind then, only that they kept me from sleep the whole damn night.

The feeling of having lost her had been awful, but to know that I had seen her and then wasted that feeling was just indescribable. I tried to console myself with the idea that the more often I saw her the more likely I was to see her again but simple words were no help to me then. I managed to get to work the next day but didn't really feel awake until my lunch hour. In the past I had always read a book during lunch but around then I had found myself walking around town instead.

I was on my way back to work and approaching the end of my hour when I saw her. Once more I was overcome and rendered numb by her presence. Amid a small group of young women she walked and talked right past me. This time she wore ragged old jeans and a black hooded sweatshirt sporting some logo or other, her companions the same. Again, all I could think of at the time was how good she looked, but moments later I was forced to consider her varying attire.

Back at work I mounted the escalator and drifted, absently up to the first floor. Stepping off I glanced over at the information desk where I spent so much of my time. My colleague had been dealing with a customer who now turned away from the desk to face me. I couldn't move. Wearing the business suit I had first seen her in, **she** walked straight towards me before heading downstairs. I watched her go, a statue agog, and didn't move until the escalator nudged a couple of customers into my back.

Having mumbled some apology, I headed for the staff room to clock in and remove my coat, my mind racing all the way. I really was beginning to doubt myself at that point, and the excitement this woman had brought to my life suddenly seemed colder and tinged with fear. Quite obviously, I couldn't believe what I had just seen and it took me almost twenty minutes of panicked thought to find the explanation.

Twins. There were two of them, one smart, one casual, twin sisters. It was obvious. I remember feeling so relieved, and so happy to have that thrill back not only intact, but heightened if anything. Subtly quizzing my workmate about the smart one I was disappointed to find that their encounter had been brief. She had tried to pay at the info desk and my colleague had directed her to the tills downstairs, that was it.

All I could think of for the rest of the day was how, had I taken my lunch at any other time, I would have spoken to her. It was that imagined conversation that led me back to wonderful sleep that night. Of course, at the time, I didn't know it would be the last real night's sleep I would ever have.

Over the rest of that week I saw them more than once each day, every time dressed differently. Despite the effect they still had on me, they really were stunning, I couldn't help but feel strange about it. I tried to convince myself that, hell, one woman's wardrobe can vary wildly enough, but between the two of them it was no wonder they were always dressed differently. This was not the only thought that nagged however.

There were their friends. I never saw either of them with the same group of people. They seemed to know everyone and yet, on occasion, I would see them walk right past people I had assumed were close friends with neither they, nor their friends, appearing to notice. I thought that, maybe those people were just friends with the other one and so tried to keep track but I quickly realised that their outfits and acquaintances were just too numerous.

While these thoughts did persist I was successful in forcing them to the fringes of my attention. These women still moved me in a quite unprecedented way with their air of grace and strength, of pure vitality. I still remembered how I had felt when I thought I would never see them again and was determined to make the most of these purely coincidental circumstances. At least that was how I felt until the end of last week.

Things changed in an instant that afternoon, just a few days ago. I was occupied behind the desk stickering stock and daydreaming of that face and form when I glanced up to find it before me. I could feel my jaw moving, trying to feel its way toward relevant speech but I had nothing.

She was just standing there, looking at me, right into my eyes. I realised that I had never once, in all those times, made eye contact. It was like seeing them for the first time all over again. I felt the most wonderful sensation of vertigo as if, at any moment, I might just tumble over into those glittering depths. She was the casual one I thought, though that line had blurred over previous days, and after a moment I realised she had spoken.

"Sorry?" I heard myself whisper, entranced.

"I'm just going on my lunch," she replied.

It was at this point that I recognised her clothes and, to my horror, her nametag. She was dressed, and addressing me, as my work colleague. Somehow the clothes managed to fit her perfectly and she even had her hair in the same style.

I looked about me briefly, hoping to spy my smirking workmates. They must have found out about my obsession and staged this elaborate stunt. There was no-one around, just me and the most beautiful woman in the world. She was still looking at me, confusion twisting her perfect features into a new and breathtaking expression. We ploughed on into strained silence until she finally broke. Her puzzlement collapsed into a smile and she shook her head.

NINE STOP TRIP

"What have you been smoking?" were the first words she ever gave me before turning and heading off to the staff room. I watched her go, still paralysed but reeling within. The moment she left my sight I stood up shakily and walked slowly from the store, deaf to question or comment. I didn't notice how cold I was without my coat but soon I was doing the unthinkable and running home.

The moment I emerged onto the street I saw her and, for a moment, I was held by the spell; but my newfound terror and confusion wrenched me free. Round the corner and there she was again, and again. I saw her six times, each dressed differently, before watching my feet carry me home faster than they had in years.

As soon as I got home I locked the door and drew all the curtains. It was just lack of sleep, I thought, it must be. With this in the tatters of my mind I went to bed and stayed there, determined to leave the waking world before I left those sheets. I spent all of last weekend in bed, ignoring the phone and knocks at the door but still I couldn't escape that beautiful face. Even if I had finally slept I know my dreams would have been full of her. As it was, I didn't sleep and got up a few days ago.

Despite finding only frustrated writhing or catatonic despair in my search for comfort I did feel somewhat rested. I pottered about behind my curtains and made myself something to eat. I had just finished when the phone rang. It would be work wanting and explanation. I had been dreading this but it was a normal and familiar dread, a thoroughly sane worry. As such I welcomed the distraction of dealing with it and answered with a quite genuinely croaking voice.

The question was expected, the voice was not. I remember feeling the cool plastic of the phone against my face drain all the warmth from my shaking form. The first time I had heard that voice it had been directed into a phone and the first time it had been aimed at me there had been both thrill and chill. Now I felt only a deep cold. I must have just dropped the phone and ran because I don't remember much directly after that.

Yesterday I found myself in the cellar, huddled under the stairs. I was cold and dirty, (I still am, not that it matters now,) but I dragged myself up to the living room. With my back flat against the wall and a shrouded window to my left I listened to several pairs of feet walk by over an hour or so before eventually finding the courage to look outside.

I heard several people on the street and so, holding my breath, I held the curtain aside with a quivering finger. After blinking in the daylight for a second or two I focussed on the pedestrians. I didn't realised I was crying until afterwards but, even through those tears, this is what I saw.

She was both halves of a couple walking hand in hand down my side of the street, minding their own business and talking quietly. Across the road and there she was wearing a policeman's uniform, making slow and deliberate progress. An elderly lady lived directly opposite and it was this door that opened now to reveal that amazing body in a dressing gown and slippers. She even made the curlers look good.

Falling back from the window I sat on the floor and, recognising the tears for the first time, continued to weep. Never in my life had I felt quite so isolated. But worse than this, I thought as sobs racked my hollow frame, I was utterly powerless and trapped within my increasingly squalid home. That was yesterday. Today I feel differently.

My curtains are still drawn and I have unplugged the phone and televisions. I still can't face them, but I have found a way out. Such was my fear before this morning that I would have just sat here and starved, but I am different now.

Last night I drank all the alcohol I could find and managed to sedate myself for a few hours. I woke quickly though and paid for the broken sleep in pain and vomit. I made it to the bathroom just in time and knelt before the toilet for several long, heaving minutes.

Eventually I managed to stand and approached the sink. Despite the shards of pain that seemed to cut through my mind I doused my fragile skull in cold water. My face dripping I straightened up a little too quickly and staggered slightly, gripping the sink for support.

Once steady I ran my hands over and over my face chasing away the water and inviting calm. My hands were at my chin as I opened my eyes and looked ahead. I was staring straight into that beautiful, terrible face; her delicate fingers just below that sickeningly perfect mouth.

I screamed.

Adam Byfield

She screamed.
Now it is over.

CUT IT OUT

The Road to The SCA: (Part 1)

Thirty-three years ago this week saw the first reported use of Hypnotic Treatment, or HypT as it subsequently became known.

Although opinion was divided at the time, this event is now recognised as the first great and important step along the road to the *'Social Conscience Act'* which is almost certain to be passed in parliament over the next few days. Initially a luxury reserved only for the super rich, HypT was dismissed by many as a passing fad.

Hypnosis had not, at this time, been recognised as the scientific discipline it is today and so still bore the old stigma of *'hocus pocus'*.

Status

As the popularity of HypT among celebrities rocketed however, it quickly became *the* status symbol of the elite.

Social commentators of the time described this as a natural progression.

Celebrities had originally used material goods, such as top of the range cars and yachts, to move themselves closer to the ideal image of the time. Times moved on and plastic surgery arrived, allowing those in the fame game to redefine their own bodies as they saw fit. The next natural step then, so it was said, was the opportunity for celebrities to reshape their minds.

Celebrity

The very earliest HypT's focussed on *neutralising* single past experiences.

The most famous, though far from the first, of these procedures was undertaken by a nineteen year old woman, winner of one of the most popular reality TV shows of the time.

The autobiography published just weeks after she was announced as the shows winner, hit the headlines almost immediately mainly due to its revelation that the young star had been raped just a few years earlier. She revealed, in an exclusive interview a few months later, that she had received HypT for the memory of the rape she put both herself and HypT firmly in the spotlight.

Creator

Focus quickly shifted from HypT's latest beneficiary to its creator, the US's Professor Anslinger. After spending almost a decade trying to publicise his discovery, Professor Anslinger now found himself invited by the world media to explain his work. The summary Anslinger gave at his first press conference still remains the most concise definition of HypT:

"The brain retains memories as factual information with emotional reposes attached. By severing this attachment to a negative memory the patient is left with full recall of the incident but

but none of the related emotional distress. The emotional memory is still there, it can simply no longer be accessed."

Progress

As the list of Anslinger's clients grew to read like a who's who of show business, HypT gained overwhelming public approval.
While hundreds of thousands of ordinary people began saving for their own HypT however, it would still be several years before the technique was officially recognised by the scientific community.
Even then however, the benefits of HypT were clear, healthier, happier people more willing and able to contribute to society. HypT wouldn't make it's real mark on the world however, until it became available to all.

Continues tomorrow...

There was a knock at the door. Kath frowned at the clock before placing the glass of pulped vegetables she had been considering grimly back on the kitchen counter. As she made her way through the newly carpeted rooms of her large and recently acquired home, the expensive clothing she wore shifted pleasantly about her.

Approaching the large and ornate front door, Kath smiled as she caught a glimpse of the exceedingly comfortable and fashionable fabric in the tall hall mirror. Taking just a moment to gather up an expression of confident ease, she opened the door.

It was yet another incredibly hot and painfully bright day. Squinting, Kath could just make out Beth, her oldest and closest friend, framed in the exquisite doorway against the backdrop of a huge and professionally maintained garden.

"Hi," they both chimed brightly.

The pair chattered comfortably as they hung Beth's coat on a gilded hook and made their way back through to the kitchen. They shared a look over the thick, dark drink Kath had left on the side before sharing a laugh. Kath put the very stylish kettle on.

A few minutes later and the two were sat sipping coffee reflectively. The air conditioning hummed subtly while the sun blazed on beyond the tightly sealed windows. Beth glanced across at her friend before biting her bottom lip, she seemed to be preparing herself.

"So what've you been up to?" Beth ventured, not quite managing to sound entirely casual. "I called over the weekend but you weren't in and then..." she paused again and her voice hardened ever so slightly. "...well you weren't at the meeting on Wednesday either."

They listened to the air con a little longer until Kath returned her mug to the table and replied. "The lottery people sent through the final amount," she explained. "Rob and I took the kids to Florida for a few days."

"Right," Beth nodded, apparently relieved. "You didn't miss much really, we were just going over the plans for the press conference again." Kath nodded absently. "Oh, there was one thing," Beth continued, trying to evoke a little more interest from her friend. "The report's going to be published early."

Kath made a non-committal noise from behind her mug, causing Beth to eye her suspiciously. "The Enquiry's report, into the abuse, the one we had to campaign for four years to have set up?" Beth was staring hard now, frowning her question.

Embarrassed recognition flushed Kath's face. "I know," she said pointedly before hiding once more behind her coffee. Beth sat back again but held her frown as she continued.

"Anyway, they've brought the report forward which is why we were going over our public response. They're releasing it next week so we'll need to be ready to make the most of whatever media attention it gets. Now you're down to speak second, if you want we can go through..."

But Kath's expression was too strange.

"What is it?" Beth asked, hoping she didn't know exactly what it was.

"About that, the press conference and everything," Kath was looking at the various luxury items and decor that surrounded her, basically anywhere except her friend's eyes. "I've just got so much going on right now, what with the last lot of money coming through and everything, I really don't think..."

Beth's jaw had actually dropped, only slightly but enough to convey her disgust quite clearly.

"What are you talking about?" she said quietly.

"Look, Beth, I've got the opportunity of a new life now, I just want to put all that behind me and get on with things, you know?"

Beth was shaking her head. "All that?" she asked, "you mean the years of systematic sexual abuse? Have you forgotten what it was like for us in that home?"

NINE STOP TRIP

"Of course not," Kath replied hurriedly. "It's just, well come one, it was all so long ago. Can't we just let it go?"

"Well you obviously can," Beth was on her feet now. "It's not just about us though, is it Kath? What about that speech you made at the last AGM, about *never again*, and *working to protect kids in care today*? Or did that all go out the window when your numbers came up?"

"That's not fair Beth," Kath said, hurt, but Beth wasn't listening, she was leaving.

Kath heard the front door slam and sat for a while longer, watching her friend's half finished coffee go cold. After a while she sighed and left the kitchen, padding slowly upstairs. She remembered those years alright and as vividly as ever.

Making her way to the master bedroom she remembered the dorms she had slept in all those nights. She could picture the darkened room, the brief play of light as one of the carers let himself in. Even now she could almost smell him, getting into her bed, hear his breathing.

She hadn't forgotten a thing, things were just different now. When she recalled those thoughts it was as if she was remembering walking to work, or peeling potatoes. The memories were there, they just felt ordinary and flat.

It was a strange sensation to be able to recall those things without all the usual feelings of fear and guilt and revulsion and pain. It was like looking at pictures of someone she didn't know.

Kath crossed her bedroom, skirting the vast bed that dominated the room and entered her walk in wardrobe.

Countless pairs of shoes occupied the floor and lower shelves. She lowered herself among them and began to move certain pairs very carefully to reveal one particular shoebox out of dozens. She was well aware that what had happened to her and Beth and the others was wrong and of course she didn't *want* it to happen to anyone else.

Retrieving the shoebox she sat with it in her lap for a moment, frowning in belated anger at the way Beth had spoken to her and made her feel. Before she'd gone to Florida Kath had fully intended to carry on working with the group upon her return, using her new found wealth to help push their cause forward.

She lifted the lid and gazed down at the box's contents. She just felt differently now. It wasn't that she didn't care, it was just that, well, she'd found since they came home she just didn't have the drive for it anymore.

Slowly, almost reverently, Kath lifted a large oblong of very white, very heavy card from the box and held it gingerly between her hands. Their campaigning was just so demanding, and relentlessly disappointing. For every inch of progress they made they had to push for a mile and Kath had realised that she just couldn't motivate herself to do it any longer.

Like she said, she had a new life now. She had more money than she knew what to do with, a great family to share it with, new house, new car, clothes, jewellery and above all she now had this. Tracing an expensively manicured nail over the embossed type she whispered the words printed on the immaculate surface.

"This document hereby certifies that, on the date entered above, the patient named below received one single course of Hypnotic Treatment[TM] at the personal clinic of Professor Anslinger, Florida, U.S.A."

The Road to The SCA: (Part 2)

Just over twelve years ago came the historic tipping point whereafter more than half the population of the nation had undergone HypT. From the highest privilege of the world's elite, to common pastime of the majority and all in just over two decades. The rise of HypT was meteoric. Having become the must have procedure of the early twenty-first century, HypT took its first step toward the masses with the opening of the first international franchise. Although still hugely expensive, HypT was now on the high street and so infinitely more accessible to the common public.

Low prices

The introduction of payment plans and credit agreements widened the crack in the doors a little wider, but it was the arrival of the so called *'budget clinics'* that threw them wide open.

Selling themselves as low cost, no frills, cheap and cheerful and various other catchy slogans, these new town centre clinics specialised in delivering fast treatment at the lowest possible price.

With the barriers of travel, cost and recovery time all removed, the use of HypT rocketed. While recognised by most as the dawn of a golden age, this development was not universally popular. HypT had attracted a great number of critics during its first few years however most of these had begrudgingly retracted their concerns as the years passed and the technique flourished.

Terrorists

There were those however who clung bitterly to the pre HypT past. Around the time that the budget clinics made their first appearance so did the, now infamous, terrorist group the G2Bs. Even when use of HypT became the majority choice, the tiny group refused to bow to democratic pressure and has fought a futile but costly war against both the state and Professor Anslinger's work ever since. Although G2Bs' best efforts had no impact whatsoever on HypT's success, a slowdown did eventually come. Pundits of the day spoke of *'market saturation'* and it was thought by many that there was simply nowhere left to go.

Next steps

During his years of phenomenal success however, Professor Anslinger had not rested on his laurels. The HypT technique itself was constantly being developed, refined and, finally, taken to another level. Historically, one of the most frustrating limitations of HypT had been the need for an individual session of treatment for each issue or memory. Although no evidence was ever found that

repeated treatments were harmful to the patients' minds, they could certainly be damaging to their bank balances. It is almost ten years since Professor Anslinger gave only his second historic press conference and unveiled his new treatment, HypT+. The beauty of the new treatment, he explained, was that rather than severing the emotional baggage from one specific memory or issue, HypT+ severed the connections to all such unwanted feelings. Just as at the birth of HypT, there was some degree of caution and concern over the safety of the technique. How could a patient be sure that they would not lose emotions they wished to keep, the Professor was asked. His response was, typically, direct and convincing.

"The decision as to which connections are kept and which are severed is made by the patients' own subconscious at every stage.
"In effect we are simply allowing the brain to cleanse itself. As one of my younger research

assistants put it, they choose what they lose.
"I should also mention that previous HypT sessions pose no barrier to this new treatment."
HypT+ was, unsurprisingly perhaps, an enormous success. Following a similar pattern to its predecessor, albeit over a much shorter time, HypT+ was the new luxury of the stars before gradually working its way down to the man on the street.

Benefits

The benefits of HypT and HypT+ can still be seen throughout society today. Whether it was the vast sums of state money saved by the elimination of traditional treatments for stress and depression, or the crime rate which fell consistently in line with the growth of these treatments, few could argue that Professor Anslinger's work hadn't changed the world for the better. But what was next for the great man?

Concludes tomorrow...

NINE STOP TRIP

A sob tore through the silence.

"He never wanted to die in hospital," said the young man, fighting every single tear. "He wanted me to take him home," here his voice broke, "and I just walked away." Now the tears came more freely as he sagged back into his chair.

Sat beside him in the small and softly furnished room, Catherine waited a few moments before speaking gently. "It's very natural for you to feel like this Alan, even though there really wasn't anything you could have done." The pair talked quietly a little while longer before both standing and approaching the door.

"I hope you've found this useful Alan," Catherine smiled up at the young man.

"I really have," he replied, taking a deep breath and visibly relaxing, "thank you so much." He extended and hand for her to shake before thinking better of it and leaning in to give her a hug. The two chatted as they made their way from the room and through the corridors of the beleaguered community centre.

Stepping into the main lobby Catherine's eyes ran over the heavy shades that obscured every window, protecting interior of the building from the searing heat without. Glancing at the clock she noted that their session had run on longer than usual and that it was now just after noon.

"Would you like a coffee or something while you wait?" She turned to Alan, nodding towards the clock.

"No, you're ok, I'm only round the corner, I'll take my chances." Alan pulled up his lined hood of metallic foil and pulled the face mask hanging about his neck up and to obscure his features.

"Are you sure?" Catherine asked, unable to keep the concern from her voice, "It's pretty bad out there today."

"I'll be alright," he said and she knew he was probably grinning behind his protective mask. Catherine opened the inner door for him and they said their goodbyes before she closed it again. A second later she heard the heavy outer door open and immediately felt the intense external heat warming the inner door.

Trying to leave her worries behind her she made her way up the stairs towards the main meeting room above. Making her way down the corridor she could hear the rumblings of an intense debate. Reaching the open doorway, Catherine leaned against the frame and surveyed the scene before asking a nearby colleague for an explanation.

"We're preparing Neil for his press conference," Janet whispered. "He's asked everyone to be as aggressive as possible and ask the most difficult questions they can think of, so he can practice."

Folding her arms Catherine nodded. "Makes sense," she replied, surveying the scene. Most of the members of their group were present she noted, but then at this time of day nobody could go anywhere anyway.

Their group had grown significantly over the

past few years. Initially providing free counselling service to the community, they had found themselves increasingly drawn into the political debate over the rise in prevalence of so called Hypnotic Treatment.

Just a few months ago, realising that no-one else seemed prepared to, they had finally given themselves a name and thrown their hat firmly into the political ring. Standing at the far end of the room, Neil was wearing one of the T-shirts they had recently managed to produce and calmly fielding each question as it came.

"Doesn't the very name of your organisation prove that your aim is to make everyone unhappy?" Neil looked down at the bold words across his chest with a wry smile: **GLAD TO BE SAD!** they shouted silently.

"Not in the slightest," he replied in a measured tone, banishing any further trace of humour from his expression. "What we, and our name, represent is the idea that there is actually some value to negative emotions and that removing them altogether is in fact incredibly dangerous."

"What about the fact that most people in this country have now undergone some form of HypT. Shouldn't you accept the majority opinion in this matter?"

"That's simply not true. Those figures," at this point Neil waved a document at the mob before him, "assume that each HypT session was performed on a different person. In fact, as we are all aware, there are a large number of people who undergo repeated sessions. HypT is not the majority choice of the nation.

"Even if it were however," he continued, "democracy is not simply majority rule. We feel we have a genuine grievance to raise and the democratically arrived at laws of this country enshrine our right to do so freely."

"Isn't it true that the crime rate has fallen month on month since HypT became publicly available. Surely this proves that HypT is making the world a better place."

Neil retrieved another document from the collection at his feet. "Yet again, this just isn't the case. If you took the time to look at the various government reports you'll see that *recorded* crime is falling but that this doesn't necessarily mean there is less crime. What's actually happening here is that crime is increasing, it's just that people are undergoing HypT rather than going to the police.

"This demonstrates our main concern over Hypnotic Treatment, namely that it encourages people to care only for themselves at society's expense. As long as they can escape the distress of being a victim of crime for example, they don't care about stopping it happening."

He had barely drawn breath before the next question arrived.

"HypT has saved the tax payer vast sums of money formerly spent on traditional treatments for depression and emotional trauma. Do you really expect the public to foot the bill for your great step backwards?"

Neil grinned at the particularly biting tone of this question and, after another quick paper shuffle, responded in his infinitely patient manner.

"Check your facts! The public spending figures for healthcare over the last century paint a very clear picture. Mental health was always the very bottom of the pile. Powerful medication was the only the form of treatment many GPs had to offer and what pastoral alternatives there were, were woefully under funded.

"In fact our organisation only came into existence to try and plug this gap by providing volunteer counsellors. The truth is that HypT has brought no savings to the tax payer because, compared to other issues, no serious money was ever spent on mental health in the first place.

"The money collectively spent on HypT on the other hand, has been astronomical and, since acquiring the status of *public service* from the government, the clinics have not been required to pay a penny of this fortune in tax. Were this decision reversed we estimate that income tax could actually be cut by between 5-10% without reducing the government's income."

The crowd muttered into silence as the questions apparently dried up. Neil was ready for his press conference. Scanning the room however, Catherine gave them a moment before calling out a question of her own.

"The HypT clinics are some of the richest and most powerful companies of all time, they have the government, the media and most of the population on their side. What makes you think you can make a difference?"

Neil squinted slightly to see where this last had come from. Spying Catherine he grinned warmly in recognition of the opportunity she was giving him. "We have something they don't," he began.

"Our work is hard. It's demanding, isolating; perpetually frustrating and disappointing and sometimes just downright depressing. We don't run away from these emotions however, we rise to their challenge, individually and as a group.

"Overcoming these obstacles makes us stronger, more resilient; it strengthens the bonds between us and drives us forward. This is what HypT takes from people, it is also why we will win."

The Road to The SCA: (Part 3)
Just three short years ago Professor Anslinger announced that he had reached what he described as the pinnacle of his research.

Thanks to HypT+'s status of public service, this new procedure of Hypnotic Surgery, or HypSur as it quickly became know, began life in the hands of the government as well as the super rich.

HypSur involved a whole new level of mental manipulation.

Breakthrough

While HypT+ had removed the existing connections between past memories and their emotional fallout, HypSur enabled the brain to avoid making these connections in the first place.

As Professor Anslinger himself explained:

"The recipient of Hypnotic Surgery gains the ability to choose, subconsciously of course, only to interact emotionally with situations they feel will be positive for them.

"Of course there is still a place for HypT+ in today's world, but it is my fervent hope that through HypSur we will one day be able to eliminate the need for HypT+ altogether."

Anslinger's dream began to take shape at an astonishing pace. The government's first application of the new procedure was to make it available through the state health system upon doctor's referral. It was not long however before it was suggested that if HypSur could make employees happier and less prone to stress and illness, it could improve the efficiency of a workforce.

The civil service set the trend that was soon followed by all the world's major companies, ie. to make HypSur a mandatory condition of employment.

This move soon drew public protests however from people concerned that a two tier state was being created, and of course there were still those extremist groups such as the G2Bs, opposing all types of Hypnotic procedure.

Equality

In response to this, and in an election year no less, the government rolled out HypSur programmes throughout the country. HypSur was made freely available to all upon request, and made mandatory for all school children.

The government also announced that as so much crime could be seen as being the result of feelings of alienation or deprivation, HypSur would be made mandatory for anyone with a criminal record and for anyone claiming benefits.

Most greeted the arrival of HypSur with joy and agreed that a new age was dawning for humanity, that sadness and bad feeling were being consigned to history forever.

Terrorists

There were still a tiny yet very vocal minority however determined to drag society back. The leader of this minority, described by government sources as a dangerous terrorist and known only as N, was executed last week after spending just over a decade in emergency detention.

The G2Bs' leader was arrested at his first and last ever press conference after which the group dramatically changed direction and began attempting to establish alternative communities away from the urban areas.

In fact nothing had been heard from the group for several years until just a few weeks ago when the government announced the Social Conscience Act.

The G2Bs, unsurprisingly, oppose the move to make HypSur universally mandatory to all citizens with no exceptions, and to all newborn babies automatically undergoing HypSur immediately after birth.

Social conscience

The Act, which is expected to be passed almost unanimously tomorrow, is the culmination of a long journey for the country and for Professor Anslinger. Step by step we have, as a nation and despite the best efforts of some, managed to put negative emotion behind us.

This Act will be the final nail in the coffin of sadness and the first step on a new journey into a bright and happy future.

A voice came from behind.

"Are you still here?"

Professor Green jumped, but tried not to show it and composed himself quickly to retort.

"No Phil, I left about half an hour ago." He didn't turn round but did continue to peer into the microscope he had been hunched over for the last three hours. Noting the latest developments in his journal, the Professor heard his assistant settling into work at his station.

There was the sound of him hanging his coat; the brief electronic chime as he logged into his computer; the hard slap of his lunch case being placed on the workbench. Every day the same he thought, pausing briefly to eye the walls of solid stone surrounding them both.

"I just meant..." Phil began, suddenly at the Professor's elbow having apparently not made any sound in crossing the floor.

"Damn it man!" The Professor jumped again, raising a slightly shaking hand to caress the frown he perpetually wore. Rising from his stool he faced his fresh faced assistant and noticed, not for the first time, how old he felt in comparison.

"What are doing back here anyway?" He snapped, "what time is it?"

Phil smiled gently, "it's seven o'clock Professor."

"Which one?" The old man rubbed at his eyes irritably.

"Morning sir, what other seven o'clock is there?"

"The evening you dolt!" The Professor's eyes were red and wet as they scowled at Phil.

"Oh," he said, understanding, "you mean 19 o'clock."

Just for a moment the Professor looked

utterly exasperated with his assistant, before bustling past him, grumbling all the way.

"Get out of my way," he said. "And do some work!" he called back as he entered his office at the far end of the lab. Phil shook his head and smiled after his boss before taking his place at the microscope and adding more numbers to the journal.

Professor Green sat down heavily behind his desk and stared at the horribly familiar walls of his office. He squinted, without much interest, at the various papers scattered before him before giving up and sitting back to stare at the ceiling.

Tracing familiar cracks he felt a familiar pull on his attention. After a few minutes he could stand it no more and slipped a small key from the pocket of his lab coat. With great care he unlocked the second drawer down in his desk and slowly opened it.

Unlike every other flat surface in the office save the floor, the interior of the drawer was not cluttered with clerical debris. In fact just a single object sat very neatly in the very centre of the drawer and it was this that the Professor lifted gingerly out and placed on the desk before him.

A simple wooden frame held an aging photograph of two happy looking people on a beach. The man in the photograph was clearly the Professor, though he had lost both significant weight and hair since it was taken. The woman next to him had piercing blue eyes that, even now, seemed to shine out from the picture.

The professor gazed down at the picture for

a few seconds, utterly still, utterly quiet, before turning his attention to the ring on his left hand. Suddenly a drop of water fell onto the glass, obscuring the woman's face.

Startled, Professor Green reached up to find his face wet. Frowning, he blustered the picture back in the drawer and locked it, returning the key to his pocket with a grim but satisfied nod. He took a deep breath just in time before Phil burst into his office, journal in hand.

"Professor!" He exclaimed.

"Yes Phil?" The Professor replied nonchalantly.

"You've..." Phil seemed at a loss, looking down into the journal apparently for advice. "I was going over your log, the tests you did last night..."

"Were you," the Professor would still not be drawn.

"But it's here! You've done it! You found it! A cure! Millions of lives!" Phil's face was deeply flushed.

"If you don't calm down Philip, you're going to faint, and frankly there's quite enough clutter in here as it is. Yes, I did make a rather significant breakthrough last night..."

"Significant! We must inform Command!" Phil blurted out, eyes wide.

"However," the Professor raised a warning finger, "it would be prudent to check our work thoroughly would it not, before we rush off to blow our trumpets for the Generals."

"But..." Phil finally seemed to be running out of steam. "Of course Professor, whatever you say." He turned and trudged back out to the lab. After few moments more the Professor followed him. They worked in concentrated silence for a while until Phil, almost petulantly, addressed the Professor.

"You don't want to leave do you?"

"Hmm?" The old man was now staring intently as his computer screen.

"Once we present a cure to Command we can go back to the surface, see the sun rise."

"Through six inches of glass," the Professor replied dismissively.

"What's an inch?" Phil asked.

"Never mind," sighed the Professor.

"We could see our families," said Phil, more to himself than to old man. The Professor stopped what he was doing and looked over at his assistant.

"You're right Phil, I'm sorry," he said finally. Phil just frowned however so he continued. "I'm being a selfish old man. Of course you want to see your family. We'll submit our findings by the end of the day, ok?" The giddy, red faced Phil returned in an instant.

"That's brilliant Professor! I'll go and message Laura right now," but he paused, as if held by an invisible bond.

"Yes, yes," said the Professor absently, waving his hand and releasing the young man. Phil was about to rush for the door but paused again at the last moment, looking over at the old man in the white coat.

"Why don't you want to go back sir?" His

face betrayed both curiosity and concern.

"Oh it's..." the Professor waved his hand once more. "...complicated," he decided on. Phil licked his lips, as if unsure how to continue.

"You could get the treatment," he ventured, his voice suddenly smaller.

"What?" The Professor asked, having apparently missed Phil's meaning.

"You know sir, you could get Hypnotic Treatment. Now that your part of the project has been completed your brain isn't *vital in its current state to national security* anymore." Phil was quoting a certificate that definitely lay somewhere within the confines of the Professor's office, though neither man would have put money on being able to find it.

"And why would I want to do that?" The Professor had turned to face Phil now and was looking directly at him. Phil shuffled slightly before continuing.

"Well sir, I know the passing of your late lady wife is still a problem for you..." the tightening of the Professor's jaw and the hardening of his eyes stopped Phil dead.

"That subject," said the old man, his tone seemingly lowering the carefully controlled temperature in the lab by several degrees, "is not up for discussion."

"Of course sir," offered Phil, clearly resisting the urge to kick himself. "Sorry sir," he added. "It's just that..." Phil continued, apparently surprising them both.

"Well..." the professor snapped, his tone no

warmer.

"Well what with the Social Conscience Act and everything, won't you sort of..." Phil squirmed, "...have to?"

"Social Conscience!" The Professor scoffed. "Those fools couldn't cobble a social conscience together between them and I'll be damned if I let them loose inside my head."

"But what will you do?" Phil seemed genuinely concerned.

"Whatever I have to I suppose," suddenly the Professor seemed to be the uncomfortable one.

"What?" The more incredulous Phil sounded the more confident he became. "You'll go out into the deserts with those, *Twobies*," he spat the last word out as if it carried a particularly unpleasant taste. "Living like an insect in the sand, wallowing in self pity?"

"I'll do," snapped the professor, interrupting and standing and reminding Phil exactly who was in charge, "as I see fit. If that's alright with you of course!" His sarcasm bit into Phil and seemed to shake him from his dogma.

There was a long and uncomfortable silence during which the Professor returned to his work while Phil was still apparently torn between the door and his boss. "I'm sorry sir, it's just that, well, you're a brilliant man, and a kind man and, well..." finally the Professor turned back to face him.

"...you're a good man. I hate to think of you being so unhappy, it just seems so unnecessary. If anyone deserves to be happy it's you." Finally Phil seemed to accept defeat and turned toward the door.

"Phil," the Professor called, making his way over to face his assistant. "You're a very thoughtful young man with makings of a first rate scientist. I know it must all seem so simple to you but think about it..." here he paused to place a hand on the young man's shoulder. "...do you really think I could have come this far if I hadn't been running away from something?"

Printed in the United Kingdom
by Lightning Source UK Ltd.
135489UK00001B/13-60/P